C000109984

Every recipe in this book includes information on:

– the **number** of servings
– the **preparation time**, including cooking times
– the **nutritional value** per portion

The following symbols are used:

■	= simple
■ ■	= more complicated
■ ■ ■	= demanding

kcal	= kilocalories
P	= protein
F	= fat
C	= carbohydrate

NB.	1 gram of protein contains about 4 kcal
	1 gram of fat contains about 9 kcal
	1 gram of carbohydrate contains about 4 kcal

All weights and measures in the book are given first in metric, then in imperial. For example: 100g/4oz or 600ml/1 pint. Always stick to the same type of measures, metric or imperial, when cooking the recipes.

g	= gram
kg	= kilogram
ml	= millilitre
l	= litre
cm	= centimetre

oz	= ounce
fl oz	= fluid ounce
lb	= pound
in	= inch

tbsp	= tablespoon (about 15g)
tsp	= teaspoon (about 5g)
pinch	= about 1g

All temperatures are given in Celsius and Fahrenheit and refer to the settings used on conventional electric ovens. The corresponding gas mark is also given.

140°C/275°F	= **Gas Mark 1**
150°C/300°F	= **Gas Mark 2**
170°C/325°F	= **Gas Mark 3**
180°C/350°F	= **Gas Mark 4**
190°C/375°F	= **Gas Mark 5**
200°C/400°F	= **Gas Mark 6**
220°C/425°F	= **Gas Mark 7**
230°C/450°F	= **Gas Mark 8**
240-250°C/475°F-500°F	= **Gas Mark 9**

– If you have a fan-assisted oven, adjust the temperatures according to the manufacturer's instructions.

– Times and settings for microwave ovens are only given in the section on microwave recipes.

Pasta, Pizza and Rice

RECIPES AND PHOTOGRAPHY

INTRODUCTION AND BASIC RECIPES

– Friedrich W. Ehlert –
– Odette Teubner, Kerstin Mosny –

HEARTY HOME COOKING

– Rotraud Degner –
– Pete Eising –

DISHES FROM AROUND THE WORLD

– Rotraud Degner –
– Ulrich Kerth –

SPECIAL OCCASION RECIPES

– Marianne Kaltenbach –
– Rolf Feuz –

WHOLEFOOD RECIPES

– Doris Katharina Hessler –
– Ansgar Pudenz –

QUICK AND EASY RECIPES

– Cornelia Adam –
– Michael Brauner –

MICROWAVE RECIPES

– Monika Kellermann –
– Odette Teubner, Kerstin Mosny –

SLIMLINE COOKERY

– Monika Kellermann –
– Anschlag & Goldmann –

Translated by UPS Translations, London
Edition edited by Josephine Bacon and Ros Cocks

CLB 4209
Published originally under the title "Das Neue Menu: Pasta, Pizza, Reis und
Korn" by Mosaik Verlag GmbH, Munich
© Mosaik Verlag, Munich
Project co-ordinator: Peter Schmoeckel
Editors: Ulla Jacobs, Cornella Klaeger, Heidrun Schaaf, Dr Renate Zeltner
Layout: Peter Pleischl, Paul Wollweber

This edition published in 1995 by Grange Books
an imprint of Grange Books PLC,
The Grange, Grange Yard, London, SE1 3AG
English translation copyright © 1995 by CLB Publishing, Godalming, Surrey
Typeset by Image Setting, Brighton, E. Sussex
Printed and Bound in Singapore
All rights reserved
ISBN 1-85627-731-3

PASTA, PIZZA AND RICE

Grange
BOOKS

Contents

Introduction

*M*any types of cereal have regained their reputation and are enjoying an increasing popularity in the kitchen. A variety of grains are being ground into flours of varying grades and are being used both in baking and for making pasta. Wholefood cookery is simply unthinkable without the use of cereal products. The reason is simple: products made from the whole grains contain more protein, vitamins, minerals – and above all more fibre – than those made from bleached, white, roller-milled flour. Pasta and pizza made from white flour do, however, remain highly popular with the consumer, and the nutritional value of these products can easily be increased by serving appropriate accompaniments.

Photo:

1. Bean threads: Strictly speaking, these are not a type of pasta. They are made from rice or soya flour and used in oriental cuisine.

2. Cannelloni: Squares of pasta rolled into tubes and filled with a meat sauce. The dish is completed by pouring sauce over it, topping it with cheese and then browning in the oven.

3. Fusilli: Corkscrew-shaped pasta, available in various lengths.

4. Farfalle: Small squares of dough which are crimped on opposite sides and gathered together in the centre. This gives them a butterfly-like shape, hence the name.

5., 6. Spaghetti: can be coloured with various natural ingredients – durum wheat combined with spinach colours the pasta green, whereas paprika makes it red. Pasta made of wholewheat is brown.

7. Lasagne: Rectangles of 4 x 7cm/1½ x 3 inches, layered alternately with Bolognese and Béchamel sauce. Lasagne made with green pasta is known as lasagne verde.

8. Penne: Short tubes, cut obliquely at the ends like quills.

9. Tortellini: Small pasta parcels, which may contain a meat, vegetable or cheese filling.

10. Ravioli: Squares of 5-8cm/2-3 inches, filled with various fillings and folded into triangles.

11. Tagliatelle: Long, narrow ribbons (20 x 0.4cm/8 x ⅜ inch), rolled into "nests".

12. Pappardelle: A kind of ribbon pasta.

CEREAL PRODUCTS

Pasta, dumplings, gnocchi and all the variations have one thing in common – in their simplest form, they consist of flour kneaded with water and/or eggs to make a dough. The dough is then cooked in salted water or stock for varying lengths of time, depending on size and whether it is freshly-made or dried.

Products made from durum wheat do not contain eggs. Egg noodles, on the other hand, must contain at least 2 – 4 eggs in 1kg/2¼ lbs pasta. For home-made egg noodle dough, 1 or 2 eggs should be used for every 100g/4oz flour.

PASTA

Pasta is a type of cereal product available in a whole variety of shapes, colours and types. It is possible to make a neutral-tasting pasta using durum wheat (grano duro) and water, without adding any further ingredients. Unlike soft wheat, hard durum wheat has a high gluten content, which is essential to the firm bite of the pasta when it is cooked *al dente*. Neutral-tasting pasta can be combined with a wide variety of Italian stews and sauces.

Every Italian region has its own pasta shapes and recipes. In southern Italy, the most popular dish is macaroni with tomatoes, aubergines and sardines, while in Tuscany, lasagne is especially popular.

DUMPLINGS AND CUT NOODLES (SPAETZLE)

Whereas pasta is typical of Italy, the cuisine of other countries is typified by various types of dumplings. In central and eastern Europe,

Potatoes for "Bubenspitzle" are pressed through a potato masher.

The potato dough is rolled into equal-sized finger shapes.

there is a type of dumpling known as *spaetzle* (cut noodles) which consists of pasta-type dough scraped or cut from a ball of dough and dropped straight into boiling water), or made into parcels and finger-sized rolls (*Bubenspitzle*). Whereas dumplings are made predominantly from potato dough, spaetzle and pasta parcels are typical egg dough products and can be made from all types of flour.

GNOCCHI

Classic gnocchi are made from polenta (cornmeal) and are known as *gnocchi alla romana*. In addition to semolina dumplings, there are also *gnocchi piemontesi*, made from potatoes, *gnocchi verdi*, made with spinach and ricotta, and *gnocchi alla parigina*, which are made with choux pastry and Parmesan cheese. Gnocchi are a meal in themselves and do not require any accompaniment. They are popular all the way from northern Italy to Rome.

Sugos, pestos, tomato sauces, gravy, grated hard cheese or herbs sautéed in olive oil all go well with gnocchi, not to mention white truffles, which are sliced finely and sprinkled over the top.

POLENTA

Polenta, cornmeal porridge, is not only a national dish in Italy. In Switzerland, especially the Tessine, the Italian-speaking region, and parts of the Balkans, a meal without it is almost unthinkable. Porridge is probably one of the oldest dishes in the world; crushed grains were cooked to make a paste soon after fire had been discovered.

The cornmeal for polenta is sold in varying grades of coarseness, and is now available in yellow and white. Making polenta requires time and patience. Polenta is an extremely versatile ingredient. It can be served in slices, perhaps with fillings, or shaped into balls; it may even be cooked in a baking tin and then unmoulded on to a serving dish. It can also be baked into puddings, pies and flans. Classic polenta is boiled in a large, deep pot over a wood fire, stirring constantly, for at least 45-50 minutes. It may be prepared using water, milk, half-water half-milk, or with stock. The cornmeal is stirred into the liquid so that no lumps form, and it must be stirred constantly until cooked. The polenta is ready when it no longer sticks to the side of the pan. It is then simply poured out on to a wooden board and divided into portions, using a wooden spatula. Hearty stews and sauces go well with polenta.

RICE

Rice is the most important cereal, being a staple food for over 50% of the world's population. As far back as 3500 B.C., rice, 'the bread of Asia', was cultivated in the area which is now known as Thailand. The ancient Greeks and Romans considered rice to be a delicacy.

Nowadays, over 8,000 different types of rice are known. Rice has become an indispensable part of our cuisine, as this popular staple can be prepared in many different ways and combined with a whole variety of ingredients. Rice has a high nutritional value and can be eaten either hot or cold, as a side-dish, in a main course, or as a dessert. Rice is ideal for slimmers, as its volume increases by up to three times due to water absorption during cooking; this makes it very filling. Its carbohydrate content gives a lasting feeling of fullness.

In addition to protein, rice contains fat and carbohydrates (fibre), valuable minerals and vitamins (above all, the B vitamins). The nutritional value of rice varies considerably, depending on how it is processed and cooked. There is a difference between white rice, brown rice, parboiled rice and pre-cooked rice. Wild rice is not strictly speaking a rice at all.

Rice can also be bought as rice flour, ground rice and rice flakes. Rice flour, for instance, is the main constituent of bean threads.

Photo: Short-grain rice (1), whole-grain rice (2), easy-cook rice (3), long-grain rice (4), parboiled rice (5), wild rice (6), long-grain brown rice (7).

NUTRITIONAL TABLE FOR RICE
Values relate to 100g/4oz rice

Rice type	kcal	P	F	C	Fibre	Minerals[1]	Vitamins B1, B2
		in grammes				in milligrammes	
Brown rice	348	7.4	2.2	75	4	175	0.5
White rice	347	7.0	0.6	78	1.4	110	0.1
Parboiled rice	345	6.5	0.5	78	1.4	119	0.5
Wild rice	87	3.5	0.2	19	1	245	1

[1]Potassium, calcium, iron

Wild Rice (Zizania aquatica) is not a rice at all, but belongs to the family of grasses. It is known as rice, due to the fact that it looks and tastes like rice and flourishes under similar conditions. Wild rice grows only in the USA and Canada. Until recently it was extremely expensive, due to the fact that it was not cultivated, and so the harvest was small. Harvesting also required intensive labour, since the Indians harvested the grains by hand. Wild rice has been cultivated since the end of the 1980s, and this has made it more affordable. Gourmets appreciate its agreeable nutty taste. It can also be mixed with long-grain rice or other cereal grains. Pecan rice is a less expensive alternative which is a true rice with the same nutty flavour as wild rice.

White rice is polished rice; the valuable bran and the germ are removed. This rice is very low in useful nutrients in fact, strictly speaking, it has no nutritional value at all.

Long-grain rice is the most commonly used rice in the West. It has a high gluten content, which is why this rice stays firm and shiny when cooked. The best long-grain rice comes from Pakistan, India, the USA, Siam, Surinam, Mexico and Thailand, and the most well-known types are Basmati and Patna. Basmati rice is the most expensive long-grain rice, and has a delicious fragrance. Long-grain rice is particularly suitable for making pilaf or creole rice and any type of Indian rice dish. Carolina rice is a cross between long-grain and short-grain rice.

Short-grain or pudding rice is used not only in sweet dishes but also to make delicious risottos, which are meals in their own right. The grain of short-grain rice is shorter but considerably thicker than that of the long-grain variety. When cooked, short-grain rice is softer and stickier than long-grain rice, as it has a lower gluten content. The main cultivation areas are China and Japan in Asia, and Spain and Italy in Europe.

Easy-cook rice is a white rice which has been pre-cooked and re-dried in a special process. It only needs to be boiled briefly before it is ready to eat. After the rice has been through a prior cooking and drying process, the cooking time is considerably shortened – to between 3 and 6 minutes, – but this does have a considerable effect on the taste of the rice which many consider to be bland and unappetising. It is mostly imported from the United States.

Brown or whole-grain rice is unpolished rice which is preferred for wholefood cooking. After harvesting, only the husks are removed, and the bran and the germ are retained. For this reason, brown rice is the most nutritious form, since the vitamins, fat, protein, minerals and fibre are preserved. It has a limited shelf life, since fat in the bran and the germ turns rancid relatively quickly. Brown rice also takes longer to cook than white rice, requiring almost twice the cooking time.

Parboiled rice is so called because it is subject to a cooking process while still in the husk. This transfers the B vitamins and some of the minerals from the husk to the grain before husking, making the grain more nutritious. It loses its yellow colour after cooking.

COOKING TIMES FOR 1 CUP (250g/8 oz) OF RICE

Type	Quantity of liquid	Cooking time	Resulting quantity of rice
Long-grain	1 3/4-2 cups	20-25 minutes	3 cups
Short-grain	1 1/2 cups	30-35 minutes	3 cups
Brown rice	2-2 1/2 cups	40-50 minutes	up to 4 cups
Parboiled rice	2-2 1/2 cups	20-25 minutes	up to 4 cups
Easy-cook rice	1-2l/ 1 3/4-3 1/2 pints	5-10 minutes	2 cups
Wild rice	4 cups	40 minutes	2 cups

CEREALS

Cereals are the most important staple of the Western world. Each grain of cereal is constructed in the same way: a thin layer surrounds the whole grain, which consists mainly of fibre; there then follows a layer of gluten, which surrounds the germ. The gluten is rich in vitamins, protein and nutritious oils, and the germ too is particularly rich in protein and fat. Finally, there is the endosperm, which is rich in carbohydrates (starch), but low in vitamins, protein and minerals. The health value of cereal is based on this composition. Cereals are grown on 60% of the world's arable land, although the majority is used as animal feed.

1. Rye is generally ground into flour, which is predominantly used to make bread. The grain is characterised by its strong flavour. In wholefood cookery, rye is used both for bread-making and for pasta.

2. Barley was one of the most important types of cereal for centuries, although it relinquished its status to wheat once bread-baking had been invented, since barley contains less gluten. In comparison with other types of cereal, barley contains a large amount of vitamin B2. Since barley swells considerably when cooked, it is a popular grain in wholefood cooking especially in the wholegrain pot barley form.

3. Wheat is the most important cereal for bread and baking. It is popular because of its high gluten content, which is what makes it the most ideal grain for use in baking. Pasta is made from a high-gluten variety of wheat called durum wheat. Wheat flakes, wheat

NUTRITIONAL TABLE FOR CEREAL
The nutritional values relate to 100g/4oz cereal

Cereal	kcal	P	F	C	Fibre	Minerals[1]	Vit. B1, B2
		in grammes				in milligrammes	
Barley	292	11	2	58	10	485	0.6
Wheat	304	11	2	60	10	549	0.2
Oats	359	13	7	61	6	440	0.7
Buckwheat	340	10	2	72	4	348	0.4
Maize	333	9	4	65	9	347	0.6
Millet	354	11	4	70	4	460	0.4
Spelt	320	12	3	63	9	473	0.4

[1] Potassium, calcium, iron.

semolina, wheat starch and wheatgerm oil are other wheat products. Wholewheat flour and wheatgerm plays an important role in a healthy diet.

4. Oats have a higher protein and fat content than other cereal types. Oat bran is also considered to be more digestible than that of other cereals. Oats have a high nutritional value. In addition to porridge, oats are used to make muesli, dumplings and soups. There is a wide variety of forms of oats, from the tiny flakes of rolled oats, through porridge oats and oat flakes, to groats and pinhead oatmeal.

5. Buckwheat is not a true cereal in botanical terms, but it is used as such. It contains very little gluten, so in baking it is often combined with other grains, but it is made into a porridge called kasha which is widely eaten through eastern Europe and western Asia. It has a strong, nutty and very distinctive taste.

6. Maize or Indian corn is a nutritious, easily digestible cereal, which may be processed in many ways. The plant is used as animal fodder, the young corn on the cob is served as a fresh vegetable, and the grains are used as

food for animals and humans. Cornflour, a highly-refined product, is an excellent thickener for puddings, soups and sauces. Corn oil is derived from the germ. Cornmeal, both yellow and white, is used in baking. Corn contains no gluten which means that raised breads cannot be made from it. It also loses its freshness very quickly. Dishes made from cornmeal need to be consumed very quickly.

7. Millet has the smallest and hardest grains of all types of cereal. The grains take about 15 minutes to cook - millet is cooked in the same way as rice – but they require more water, as they swell considerably. Millet is easily digestible and rich in vitamins and minerals.

8. Spelt is a primitive form of wheat formerly grown almost exclusively in south Germany and Switzerland. It is very hardy but lower yielding than other wheat varieties. The grain has a lower gluten content than wheat and is thus easily tolerated by cœliacs (people allergic to gluten), which is why spelt is now becoming available as flour, in pasta and less commonly in whole grains. It can mainly be found in healthfood shops.

9. Spelt grains are harvested early while still green, and oast-dried. They are used like cracked wheat in cereal dishes and can be ground coarsely. If you cannot find them, use cracked wheat or bulgar wheat.

CEREAL SPROUTS

Sprouts have a higher vitamin and mineral content than the grains themselves. For this reason, they are an ideal source of vitamins, above all in the winter months. They are becoming more and more popular in modern cookery as an ingredient in salads, soups, and as a vegetable dish.

It is possible to germinate sprouts at home from seeds. Rye, barley, wheat, oats and millet can all be sprouted: the temperature should be between 18°C and 22°C. The sprouting grains should not be exposed to direct light, and they need a high degree of humidity while germinating. They must be rinsed thoroughly once or twice a day while growing, preferably in a fine sieve. Various equipment may be purchased for germinating grains or pulses, but basically it is sufficient to have a jam jar sealed with a cap made of permeable fabric (such as a piece of muslin).

TYPES OF CHEESE USED FOR PIZZA AND PASTA

Pasta and pizza are simply unimaginable without cheese. Each region of Italy produces and sells its own types; the individual taste of the cheese is determined by the degree of maturity and the season in which it is made. Thanks to modern distribution methods, almost all the Italian cheeses are available outside Italy.

The information given below offers a few words about the most important varieties of cheese suitable for toppings and fillings, many of which are Italian.

1. Beaufort is a French hard cheese with a 50% fat content which melts very well. The whole cheeses themselves weigh between 30kg/66lbs and 60kg/130lbs, and contain small, round, unevenly distributed holes.

2. Cantal is a French semi-hard cheese, very similar to Cheddar, which contains 45% fat and tastes slightly bitter. It is well-suited for melting, but Cheddar can always be substituted.

3. Emmental is made from unpasteurised milk, contains 45% fat, and was originally only made in Emmental, in Switzerland. Small, round holes indicate a sharp flavour, while long, oval holes denote a mild taste. The nutty flavour develops during storage. The fully ripened cheese is very well suited for grilling and as a flavouring ingredient for rice and pasta dishes.

4. Gorgonzola is a full-fat blue cheese made from cow's milk. It is used for sauces and fillings and for adding flavour to pasta dishes.

5. Gruyère is produced in western Switzerland from unpasteurised cow's milk. It is ivory-coloured, 45% fat and is suitable for grilled toppings and for adding flavouring.

6. Parmesan, or Grana, is the classic extra-hard cheese, ideal for grating and seasoning. Parmesan is considered the king of Italian cheeses, of which the best are stored for more than 4 years. It scarcely melts when heated and thus does not become stringy. Parmesan should preferably be used freshly grated.

7. Pecorino is an extra-hard cheese with a 45% fat content, mainly produced from sheep's milk. It is sold both with and without added pepper. Pecorino's flavour does not develop until the cheese has matured.

8. Ricotta moliterno and **9. Ricotta dolce.** Curd cheeses made from whey, particularly suitable for fillings, and low in fat.

Provolone is another Italian cheese with a 45% fat content which is mainly used in grated form. There are two types, Provolone dolce and Provolone piccante; the latter has a sharp flavour which goes well with pasta.

10. Fontina is a semi-hard Italian cheese from the Val d'Aosta in northern Italy. It has a fat content of 45%, and is popular in hot dishes. Fonduta, a typical accompaniment to pasta and rice, is prepared from Fontina and cream or milk.

11. Mozzarella is made from cow's milk or buffalo milk and shaped by hand. It is commonly used for pizza, particularly in Naples. However it also goes well with pasta.

MAKING YOUR OWN PASTA
(Basic recipe for pasta dough)

1. Sift 200g/7oz strong plain or strong wholewheat flour onto a work surface and make a well in the centre. Drop 5 egg yolks, 1 tbsp olive oil and a pinch of salt into the well.

2. Mix the flour with the other ingredients and knead until the dough is smooth.

3. Shape the dough into a smooth ball, wrap in cling-film and leave to stand for 1 hour in a cool place.

4. Using either a pasta-making machine or a rolling pin, roll out the dough into thin sheets and cut to the desired widths.

5. Add 1-2 tbsps oil to boiling salted water, then add the pasta and cook for 40-60 seconds (6-8 minutes for dried pasta).

6. Pour the cooked pasta into a colander and rinse with cold water.

7. Re-heat the cooked pasta with a little water and 15g/½oz butter, seasoning with salt and nutmeg.

THE RIGHT WAY TO COOK PASTA

Pasta should always be cooked in a generous quantity of water. 1 litre/1¾ pints of water and 1 tsp salt should be allowed for every 100g/4oz dried pasta. The cooking time of the pasta will depend on its quality and the way in which it has been made. Home-made, fresh pasta requires only 40-60 seconds cooking, while home-dried pasta or commercially prepared dry pasta have a cooking time of 8-16 minutes, depending on the time indicated on the package. Cooked pasta should always be al dente, i.e. cooked but firm. When you bite through it, the centre of the pasta should still be white. Wholewheat pasta should be cooked for less time than pasta made from white flour, in order to retain the vitamins and minerals.

The quantity of pasta needed per person will vary depending on whether the pasta is to be served as an hors d'oeuvre, main course or accompaniment.
A single portion should be calculated as follows:
20-30g/¾-1oz added to soups
60-100g/2-4oz as an hors d'oeuvre
100-150g/4-5½oz as an accompaniment
200-300g/7-10oz as a main course

Wholewheat pasta should be cooked in a generous quantity of water for 10-15 minutes.

GNOCCHI ALLA ROMANA

1. Place 600ml/18 fl oz milk and 25g/1oz butter in a pan and bring to the boil. Season with salt, white pepper and grated nutmeg.

2. Once the butter has melted and the milk is boiling, pour in 100g/4oz semolina and stir until smooth.

3. Stirring constantly with a wooden spoon or metal spatula, boil the mixture for 6-8 minutes or until the semolina has thickened and cooked through.

4. Remove the pan from the heat, add 2 egg yolks and 1 egg and mix together well.

5. Return the pan containing the semolina to the stove and boil vigorously, stirring constantly, until the eggs have bound the mixture together.

6. Place the dough on a Swiss roll tin rinsed with water, smoothing it out over the tray using a palette knife until it forms a layer about 2cm/³/4 inch thick.

7. Brush the surface with 30g/1oz melted butter and sprinkle with 3 tbsps Parmesan. Leave to cool.

8. Using a circular pastry cutter 6cm/2¼ inches in diameter, cut out half-moon shapes and arrange them in an oven-proof dish.

9. Bake in a preheated oven at 250°C/475°F/Gas Mark 9 until golden brown.

In Italy, this type of gnocchi is served without an accompaniment as an hors d'oeuvre, but it is equally possible to serve it with a meat or tomato sauce.

GNOCCHI ALLA PIEMONTESE

SERVES 4
Preparation time: 50 minutes

1kg/2¼ lbs floury potatoes
15g/¹/2oz butter
1 tsp salt
¹/4 tsp grated nutmeg
1 egg
300g/10oz strong plain flour

PLUS:
50g/2oz butter
a few sage leaves or
rosemary leaves
50g/2oz freshly-grated
Parmesan

1. Do not peel the potatoes. Boil them for about 30 minutes.
2. Peel and mash the potatoes, then mix them with the butter and salt. Return them to the heat and allow to dry a little. Then transfer the mashed potatoes to a bowl and mix in the nutmeg, egg and the flour.
3. With hands coated in flour, shape the potato dough into finger-thick sausage shapes. Cut these into 2cm/³/4 inch lengths, flattening each piece slightly with a fork or index finger. The gnocchi can also be shaped into small oval dumplings, using two teaspoons.
4. Bring a generous quantity of salted water to the boil in a large saucepan. Place the gnocchi in the water, reduce the heat and simmer very gently for 6-8 minutes. As soon as the gnocchi float to the surface, remove them with a slotted spoon, drain and place in a heated dish.
5. Melt the butter in a pan. Then add the sage or rosemary and toss in the butter. Pour the butter over the gnocchi immediately and sprinkle with Parmesan.

COOKING POLENTA

1. Bring 1l/1¾ pints water or stock to the boil in a saucepan. Season with salt.

2. Pour 320g/10½oz medium-ground cornmeal into the boiling liquid and stir until smooth.

3. Stirring constantly with a wooden spoon or long wooden stick, cook the polenta for 40-45 minutes or until smooth and thick.

4. Stir 40g/1½oz butter and 50g/2oz freshly-grated Parmesan thoroughly into the polenta.

5. Rinse a Swiss roll tin with water, pour the polenta over it and spread it out using a palette knife until the polenta is about 2cm/¾ inch thick. Leave to cool.

6. Use a sharp knife to slice the polenta into rectangles measuring about 5 x 7cm/ 2 x 2¾ inches, or cut out circles about 6cm/2½ inches in diameter using a glass or biscuit-cutter

7. Fry the polenta slices in 30g/1oz melted butter until golden brown.

PLAIN POLENTA

The plainest type of polenta is made purely from cornmeal and water and is served as an accompaniment.
Different types of cheese, stirred into the polenta either individually or in combination, add special flair to the dish and transform it into a main course.

Thus, for example, it is possible to combine Fontina and Parmesan with the cooked polenta by dicing the Fontina and stirring it into the cornmeal after it has been cooked for 30 minutes. Cook the mixture for about 10 minutes more before adding freshly grated Parmesan.

Freshly grated Parmesan combined with Fontina adds a spicy touch to polenta.

MAKING PIZZA DOUGH
(Basic recipe)

1. For 4 x 30cm/12 inch bases. Sift 500g/1lb 2oz strong plain flour into a bowl and make a well in the centre. Dissolve the yeast in 3 tbsps water containing a pinch of sugar, pour the liquid into the well, mix with a little flour, and leave to rise for 20 minutes.

2. Add a further 200ml/6 fl oz lukewarm water, 10g/⅓oz salt and 3 tbsps olive oil, kneading to make a smooth dough.

3. Divide the pizza dough into four equal-sized pieces and shape each into a ball. Place the balls in a bowl, cover with a cloth and leave to rise for about 30 minutes at room temperature.

4. When the dough balls have risen, flatten them a little and roll them out into 4 thin bases, each 30cm/12 inches in diameter. The dough should be smooth and not sticky.

5. Grease two baking sheets or Swiss roll tins with oil and arrange the pizza bases on them. Make several holes in the dough, using a fork, and slightly raise the edges of the dough. A quiche dish of suitable diameter may also be used.

6. Top the pizza base with ingredients as desired. It should always be topped with cheese.

MAKING QUICHE DOUGH
(Basic recipe)

1. Sift 300g/10oz strong plain flour into a deep bowl and use a tablespoon to make a well in the centre. Add two eggs, a generous pinch of salt, and dot with 150g/5½oz tiny pieces of ice-cold butter.

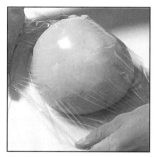

2. Knead the flour with the other ingredients to make a smooth dough.

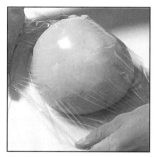

3. Shape the dough into a ball, wrap in clingfilm and leave to stand in the refrigerator for about 1 hour.

4. Use a pastry brush to grease a shallow flan case about 26cm/10½ inches in diameter, or 10 miniature flan cases each 10cm/4 inches in diameter, with melted butter, making sure the edges are well-coated.

5. Roll the dough out thinly until it is the right size for the dish. A springform tin may be used instead of a flan case. Line the tin with the rolled-out dough, pricking it several times with a fork.

6. If baking blind is indicated in the recipe, weigh the dough down with uncooked beans or rice and bake in a preheated oven at 200°C/400°F/Gas Mark 6.

COOKING RICE

1l/1¾ pints water and about 10g/¼oz salt are required to cook 100g/4oz rice. Husked rice requires a cooking time of 16-18 minutes, while unhusked (whole) rice needs about 40-45 minutes. Rice should be cooked al dente (so it is firm to bite). After cooking, the rice should be rinsed immediately in cold water and drained in a colander.

Unused cooked rice may be frozen or served fried at a subsequent meal.

The following quantities of uncooked rice should be calculated per portion:
10-15g/¼-½oz for adding to soups
40-50g/1½-2oz as an accompaniment
80-100g/3-4oz as a main course

COOKING WHOLE GRAINS

Whole grains may be used in various dishes or, like rice, they may be served as an accompaniment.

Some types of grains need soaking before cooking. It is best to soak grains for several hours before cooking in double their volume of water. The cooking times for pre-soaked and unsoaked grains are as follows:

Millet: 15-20 minutes, unsoaked
Buckwheat: 20-30 minutes, unsoaked
Rye: 1½ hours, pre-soaked
Wheat, spelt, oats, barley: 1 hour, presoaked

PREPARING RISOTTO

1. Sauté 2 tbsps finely chopped onion in 30g/1oz melted butter or 2 tbsps olive oil until transparent.
2. Add 400g/14oz Italian risotto rice and continue to sauté for a further 2 minutes. Add 250ml/8 fl oz white wine and allow to evaporate.
3. Stirring frequently using a

1

2

Some types of grain have to be soaked in water for several hours before cooking.

wooden spoon, gradually add about 1l/1¾ pints seasoned hot stock. Cook the risotto for 15-18 minutes until al dente.
4. Season the risotto with salt, pepper and nutmeg. Finally stir 40g/1½oz butter, cut into pieces, and 50g/2oz freshly-grated Parmesan into the risotto using a carving fork.

3

4

RISOTTO WITH VEGETABLES

Using a variety of vegetables, risotto can be turned into a variety of imaginative dishes. Risotto with asparagus, for instance, makes a sophisticated variation: Use 500g/1lb 2oz cooked asparagus to 200g/7oz rice. Cut the asparagus into 2cm/¾ inch lengths and sauté it in butter for about 5 minutes. The asparagus is then stirred into the rice just before it has finished cooking and the whole risotto is cooked for a further few minutes until ready for serving. The dish is served as a main course.

A WILD RICE DISH

1. Wash 120g/5oz wild rice and soak it in warm water for 2 hours. Drain well.
2. Sauté 100g/4oz diced onion, carrots and celery in 30g/1oz butter until soft. Add the rice and continue to sauté the mixture until the rice is shiny.
3. Pour 500ml/16 fl oz boiling chicken stock over the mixture and season with salt, pepper and nutmeg. Bring to the boil, then place in a preheated oven at 190°C/375°F/Gas Mark 5 and cook for 40 minutes.
4. Wash and chop two sprigs of parsley and 250g/8oz mushrooms. Using a meat fork, stir 30g/1oz butter into the boiling hot rice. Add the parsley and mushrooms and bake for another 10 minutes.

PREPARING PILAF RICE

1. In a flameproof casserole with a tight-fitting lid, sauté 2 tbsps finely chopped onions in 15g/½oz butter until transparent, then add 300g/10oz long-grain rice and continue to sauté until this, too, is transparent.
2. Pour over just under 500ml/16 fl oz stock and season with salt, white pepper and grated nutmeg.
3. Lard an onion with a small piece of bay leaf and 2 cloves, add to the rice and bring to the boil.
4. Cover the rice, place in a preheated oven and cook at 220°C/425°F/Gas Mark 7 for 16-18 minutes.
5. Gently stir 15g/½oz butter, cut into pieces, into the rice using a carving fork.

*T*here is nothing new about using dumplings, grains and noodles in cooking, even though nowadays they are enjoying renewed popularity. Dumplings and cut noodles were once widely enjoyed throughout Britain but they have waned in popularity, even though it was the British who introduced the dumpling cooked in a cloth (the Scots' cloutie dumpling) into the cuisine of Germany.

Savoury tarts and flans are also popular cereal dishes. In the wine-growing areas of Europe, onion tarts are popular accompaniments to new wine; small, spicy bacon tarts taste best with beer. This type of delicious home cooking goes back generations, and embraces a vast repertoire of cereal dishes ranging from modest snacks to Sunday lunches.

Onion Tart
(see recipe on page 37)

POTATO DUMPLINGS

SERVES 4   ■ ■

*Preparation and cooking
time: 1 hour 30 minutes
Kcal per portion: 380
P = 11g, F = 6g, C = 70g*

FOR THE POTATO DOUGH:
*1.5kg/3¼ lb raw potatoes,
   peeled
500g/1lb 2oz day-old boiled
   potatoes
250ml/8 fl oz milk
1 tbsp salt*

FOR THE FILLING:
*1 day-old white roll
15g/½ oz butter*

PLUS:
*salt
1 tbsp finely chopped chives
   (optional)*

*Wrap the raw potato in a linen
cloth and squeeze out the liquid.*

*Make a hollow in each dumpling,
place the roasted cubes of bread
in the centre and close the dough
over the top.*

1. To make the potato dough, grate the raw potatoes into a bowl filled with cold water.
2. Wrap the grated potato in a linen cloth or place it in a cloth bag and squeeze out thoroughly, retaining the liquid. Once the potato starch has settled, pour off the liquid.
3. Grate the boiled potatoes in the same way. Heat the milk, pour it over the boiled potatoes and stir until smooth.
4. Mix together the raw potato, the cooked potato mixture, the starch and salt to make a smooth, soft dough.
5. To make the filling, cut the bread roll into small dice and fry it in the butter until golden-brown.
6. Using wet hands, make dumplings of the desired size from the potato dough, placing a few pieces of diced bread in the centre of each before shaping them.
7. Bring a generous quantity of water to the boil in a large, wide saucepan, using 1l/1¾ pints water to 2 tsps salt.

Carefully place the dumplings in the water. Simmer, uncovered, for 15-20 minutes, ensuring that the water does not boil vigorously.
8. Remove the potato dumplings with a slotted spoon, drain well and place in a preheated dish.
The cooked dumplings may be sprinkled with finely chopped chives. Serve as an accompaniment to roast pork, pot-roast, or roast duck or goose.

COLOURFUL VEGETABLE FLAN

SERVES 8-12   ■ ■

*Preparation and cooking
time: 1 hour 30 minutes
Rising time:1 hour 30
minutes
Kcal per portion, to serve 8:
665
P = 16g, F = 41g, C = 54g*

FOR THE DOUGH:
*500g/1lb 2oz strong plain
   flour
½ tsp salt
20g/¾oz fresh yeast
250ml/8 fl oz lukewarm milk
80g/3oz butter*

FOR THE TOPPING:
*300g/10oz frozen spinach,
   thawed
250g/8oz carrots
100g/4oz butter
250g/8oz cauliflower
1 small onion
250g/8oz mushrooms
1 cooked beetroot
1 leek
salt
¼ tsp freshly ground white
   pepper
¼ tsp freshly grated nutmeg
250ml/8 fl oz double cream
250ml/8 fl oz milk
4 eggs*

PLUS:
*fat for the baking sheet
flour for the work surface
50g/2oz melted butter for
   coating*

1. To make the dough, mix the flour and salt in a bowl. Make a well in the centre. Crumble the yeast into the well and stir in half of the milk. Cover and leave to rise in a warm place for 15 minutes.
2. Knead the dough with the remaining milk and the melted butter, until the dough is smooth and no longer sticks to the sides of the bowl. Cover and leave to rise for 1 hour in a warm place.
3. For the topping, chop the thawed spinach. Scrape the carrots (or peel them thinly, if they are older), wash and slice thinly.

4. Heat 30g/1oz butter in a saucepan, add the carrots while they are still wet from washing, cover and sauté until they are almost cooked. Wash the cauliflower, divide it into small florets and boil in salted water until almost cooked. Peel and dice the onion, then fry it in 30g/1oz butter until transparent. Add the spinach and braise. Clean and slice the mushrooms, then fry them for a few minutes in 30g/1oz butter. Cut the beetroot first into slices and then into strips. Slice the leek into thin rings, then sauté in the remaining butter for a few minutes, cover and cook almost completely. Season all the vegetables with salt, pepper and nutmeg.
5. Preheat the oven to 200°C/400°F/Gas Mark 6.
6. Roll out the dough on a floured board, then place it on a greased baking sheet, raising it at the edge so that no liquid can escape. Leave to stand for 10 minutes.
7. Brush the dough with the melted butter and arrange perpendicular or diagonal strips of the different vegetables across it.
8. Combine the cream and milk, add the eggs, and whisk the mixture until it is frothy. Season with salt, pepper and nutmeg and distribute evenly over the vegetables, ensuring that no pieces of vegetable protrude above the topping.
9. Place the vegetable flan on the centre shelf of the oven and bake for about 40 minutes. Tastes best when lukewarm.

CAULIFLOWER FLAN

SERVES 6 ■

Preparation and cooking time: 1 hour 10 minutes
Kcal per portion: 665
P = 11g, F = 58g, C = 19g

300g/10oz frozen puff dough
1 large cauliflower
150g/5¹/₂oz mushrooms
150g/5¹/₂oz smoked streaky
  bacon
30g/1oz butter
2 tbsps chopped parsley
salt
freshly ground black pepper
flour for the work surface
4 eggs
250ml/8 fl oz cream

1. Thaw the puff dough for 20 minutes.
2. Divide the cauliflower into tiny florets. Slice the mushrooms and dice the bacon.
3. Sauté the cauliflower florets for a few minutes in 15g/¹/₂oz butter, pour over half a cup of water, and steam until almost soft. Sauté the mushrooms and the bacon in the remaining butter. Season the cauliflower and mushroom mixture with parsley, salt and pepper, then leave to cool.
4. Preheat the oven to 225°C/425°F/Gas Mark 7. Rinse a 26-cm/10¹/₂ inch springform tin in cold water.
5. Roll out the dough on a floured work surface, line the springform tin with it and bake for 15 minutes.
6. Remove the springform tin from the oven and arrange the vegetables over the pastry. Stir the eggs and cream together thoroughly, season lightly and pour over the vegetables.
7. Bake the flan on the centre shelf of the oven for 30-40 minutes or until golden brown.
Recommended wine:
dry white wine, such as Silvaner or Riesling.

MINCED MEAT FLAN

SERVES 6-8 ■

Preparation and cooking time: 1 hour 30 minutes
Kcal per portion, serve 6: 585
P = 27g, F = 41g, C = 22g

300g/10oz frozen puff pastry
1 onion
30g/1oz butter
50g/2oz cooked ham
100g/4oz minced pork
150g/5¹/₂oz finely minced
  lean beef
2 tomatoes
1 tsp tomato purée
salt
freshly ground black pepper
grated nutmeg
3 tbsps flour
3 eggs
250ml/8 fl oz milk
200g/7oz Emmental cheese,
  freshly grated

1. Thaw the puff pastry for 20 minutes.
2. Meanwhile, peel the onion and dice finely. Heat the butter in a large pan, add the diced onion and fry until transparent. Dice the ham finely and mix well with the minced pork and beef. Place in the pan and fry for a few minutes, stirring regularly.
3. Blanch and skin the tomatoes, then chop them finely. Add them to the pan with the tomato purée. Continue frying for a few more minutes – the meat should still be pink. Season with salt, pepper and nutmeg. Remove from the heat and leave to cool.
4. Preheat the oven to 225°C/425°F/Gas Mark 7. Take a springform tin 24cm/9 inches in diameter and rinse it with cold water.
5. Roll out the pastry and use it to line the bottom and sides of the springform tin. Spread the meat filling over it.
6. Place the flour in a bowl and stir the eggs in thoroughly. Gradually add the

Add the minced pork, minced beef and ham to the onions once they have turned transparent, continuing to fry for a few more minutes.

Stir the tomatoes into the meat mixture.

Stir the cheese into the sauce and pour the meat filling over it.

milk, stirring constantly, until the ingredients are well mixed. Stir in the cheese, season generously with salt and pepper, then pour the mixture evenly over the meat filling. Place the flan on the centre shelf of the oven and bake for 30-40 minutes or until golden brown.
Accompaniment:
lamb's lettuce salad.
Recommended drink:
beer.

BREAD DUMPLINGS

SERVES 4 ■ ■

Preparation and cooking time: 1 hour
Kcal per portion: 450
P = 19g, F = 13g, C = 62g

10 day-old white rolls
¹/₂ tsp salt
250ml/8 fl oz milk
15g/¹/₂oz butter
1 small onion
2 tbsps chopped parsley
4 eggs

1. Slice the rolls thinly, place them in a bowl and add the salt. Heat the milk gently and pour it over the sliced bread.
2. Heat the butter in a pan. Peel the onion, chop it finely and sauté in the pan with the parsley. Add to the bread. Then add the eggs and knead the mixture thoroughly. Leave to stand for 10 minutes.

> **TIP**
>
> *Any left-over bread dumplings can be stored in the refrigerator and eaten the next day – sliced, coated in breadcrumbs, and fried in oil on both sides until crispy. May be served with salad.*

3. Bring a generous quantity of salted water to the boil in a pan. Using wet hands, shape dumplings from the dough, place them in the water and cook for 20 minutes. Remove the cooked dumplings with a slotted spoon and place in a preheated dish.
Serve with roast veal and roast pork, ham or sausage with sauerkraut, or mushroom sauce.

VEGETABLE BAKE

SERVES 8 ■■
Preparation time:
1 hour 15 minutes
Kcal per portion: 455
P = 11g, F = 30g, C = 31g

150g/5¹/2 oz green beans
¹/2 fennel bulb
1 red pepper
250g/8oz baby carrots
salt
1 untreated orange
1 untreated lemon
200g/7oz butter
6 eggs
2 tsps celery salt
250g/8oz strong plain flour
20g/³/4 oz fresh yeast

PLUS:
butter for greasing
2 tbsps flour for sprinkling in
the baking tin and for
dusting
40g/1¹/2oz blanched almonds

1. Top, tail and string the beans, and trim the fennel bulb. Wash the beans and the fennel and chop both finely. Discard the stem, white inner flesh and seeds of the pepper, wash, dry and dice finely.
2. Blanch the fennel, beans and pepper in boiling salted water for 3 minutes, rinse in cold water and drain in a colander. Clean and wash the carrots, then dice them finely. Blanch likewise in boiling salted water for 6 minutes, then rinse and drain.
3. Dry the vegetables on two plates lined with absorbent paper.
4. Meanwhile, peel the orange and lemon in wafer-thin layers, cutting each piece of peel into fine strips. Blanch for 10 seconds in boiling water and dry on absorbent paper.
5. Cream the butter with the eggs and celery salt in a large bowl. Add the flour, the crumbled yeast and the strips of orange and lemon peel, kneading the mixture to make a soft dough.

6. Butter a large Swiss roll tin (30cm/12inches by 25cm/10 inches) and sprinkle with 1 tbsp of flour. Preheat the oven to 200˚C/400˚F/Gas Mark 6.
7. Stir the other tbsp of flour into the vegetable mixture and place it in the bowl with the dough. Gently and carefully fold the vegetables into the dough. Fill the Swiss roll tin with the mixture and scatter the almonds over the top.
8. Bake the dish on the lower shelf of the oven for 25 minutes, then reduce the temperature to 150˚C/300˚F/Gas Mark 2, cover the tin with aluminium foil, and bake for another 25 minutes. Allow to cool on a wire rack before removing from the tin and unmoulding on to a plate.
Accompaniment:
Horseradish sauce or crème fraîche mixed with herbs
Recommended wine: a dry, full-bodied Riesling.

TIP

This is a great summertime meal idea; it tastes good when cold and is easy to transport, on a picnic, for instance, since the vegetables are held in a firm dough.

Dice the carrots and add them to the other finely-chopped vegetables.

Gently fold the vegetables into the dough.

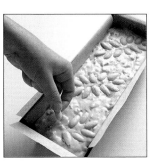
Before placing in the oven, decorate the bake with skinned almonds.

ONION TART

SERVES 8-12 ■■
Preparation time:
1 hour
Rising time:
1 hour 20 minutes
Kcal per portion, to serve 8:
570
P = 13g, F = 31g, C = 55g

FOR THE DOUGH:
500g/1lb 2oz strong plain flour
1 tsp salt
20g/³/4oz fresh yeast
250ml/8 fl oz lukewarm milk
60g/2oz butter
fat to grease the baking sheet

FOR THE TOPPING:
1kg/2¹/4 lb onions
150g/5¹/2oz streaky bacon
3 eggs
250ml/8 fl oz sour cream
salt, black pepper
1 tsp caraway seeds

1. Mix the flour and salt in a bowl, make a well in the centre, crumble in the yeast and stir in 125ml/4 fl oz milk. Cover and leave to rise for 20 minutes.
2. Melt the butter in the remaining milk, add to the dough and knead until it is smooth and no longer sticks to the bowl. Cover and leave to rise in a warm place for 1 hour.
3. Slice the onions into rings. Dice the bacon and fry until transparent. Add the onion rings and sauté until they are also transparent.
4. Whisk the eggs and the sour cream in a bowl, adding the salt, pepper and caraway seeds. Once the onion rings have cooled, combine them with the egg-and-cream mixture.
5. Preheat the oven to 200˚C/400˚F/Gas Mark 6.
6. Roll out the dough, then place it on a greased baking sheet. Distribute the bacon and onion mixture over the dough, and bake on the centre shelf of the oven for 35-40 minutes.
Recommended wine: a young white wine from England, Switzerland or Austria.

Dishes from Around the World

Naturally, Italian cuisine features prominently in this section. No other country has exported its gastronomy so successfully, although it is true to say that pizza was turned into a world-famous dish by the Americans. The innumerable types and shapes of pasta, also widely available outside Italy, inspire pasta enthusiasts to develop their own creations. In many progressive kitchens, home-made pizza, made with fresh ingredients depending on season and market availability, is replacing the commercially produced deep-frozen pizzas with their monotonous toppings. Italy has also made a priceless contribution in terms of rice dishes too, with imaginative risotto recipes surpassed only by the rice dishes of the Orient.

Indian Lemon Rice
(see recipe on page 49)

SPAGHETTI WITH PESTO SAUCE

SERVES 4 ■
Preparation and cooking time: 45 minutes
Kcal per portion: 770
P = 20g, F = 41g, C = 75g

2 potatoes
50g/2oz very tender green
  beans
40g/1¼oz salt
400g/14oz spaghetti

FOR THE PESTO:
handful of pine kernels
handful of fresh basil
  leaves
4 garlic cloves
10g/¼oz coarse sea salt
30g/1oz Parmesan
30g/1oz Pecorino
8 tbsps olive oil

The pine kernels can be dry-roasted in a frying-pan or on a baking sheet.

Crush the pine kernels, garlic, salt, basil leaves and cheese finely in a pestle and mortar.

1. To make the pesto, roast the pine kernels in a dry frying-pan until they begin to give off their aroma. Allow to cool and then chop finely.
2. Wash the basil leaves, pat them dry and cut into thin strips with a pair of scissors. Peel the garlic cloves and chop them finely.

> ## TIP
> *To freeze pesto, use only 2 garlic cloves, 30g/1oz cheese and 4 tbsps oil. Add the other ingredients after thawing.*

3. Crush the pine kernels and the chopped garlic in a pestle and mortar. Then add the basil leaves and salt, crushing them with the other ingredients.
4. Crumble the cheese, add to the mortar and crush completely. Gradually add the olive oil until a creamy mass is formed, and leave to marinate.
5. Meanwhile, peel the potatoes and dice them finely. Wash the beans and cut them into pieces.
In a large pan, bring 4l/7 pints of salted water to the boil, add the diced potato and beans and boil for 5 minutes. Then add the spaghetti and cook for 8-11 minutes or until al dente. Pour it into a sieve and drain it , reserving some of the cooking water.
6. Add a few tbsps of the cooking water to the pesto just to make it smooth. Arrange the pasta and the vegetables in a preheated dish; combine them thoroughly with the pesto.
Recommended wine:
a dry Italian red wine, preferably Rossere di Dolce-acqua (from Liguria) or Barbera.

BAKED PASTA ROLLS WITH MEAT AND SPINACH FILLING

SERVES 4 ■ ■
Preparation and cooking time: 1 hour 30 minutes
Standing time:
20 minutes
Kcal per portion: 900
P = 56g, F = 37g, C = 86g

400g/14oz strong plain flour
4 eggs
or
12 shop-bought cannelloni
1 tbsp oil
salt

FOR THE FILLING:
300g/10oz cooked meat
100g/4oz cooked ham
100g/4oz cooked spinach,
  drained and finely chopped
2 eggs
50g/2oz freshly grated
  Parmesan
salt
freshly ground black pepper

FOR THE BECHAMEL SAUCE:
40g/1½oz butter
40g/1½oz flour
500ml/16 fl oz milk
salt
freshly grated nutmeg

PLUS:
butter for the oven dish and
  for dotting over the top
50g/2oz freshly grated
  Parmesan

1. To make the dough, place the flour on a work surface, make a well in the centre and crack the eggs into it. Knead briskly by hand to make a smooth dough. Wrap in a damp cloth and leave to stand for 20 minutes.
2. For the filling, mince the cooked meat and the ham finely in a food processor. Place in a bowl and combine with the well-drained spinach. Add the lightly beaten eggs and the Parmesan.

Season with salt and pepper and stir to make a firm paste.
3. Cut the dough into 2-3 pieces. Using a pasta-making machine or a rolling pin, roll it out as thinly as possible. Use a sharp knife to cut out squares 10cm/ 4 inches in diameter.
4. Bring a generous quantity of salted water, containing 1 tbsp oil, to the boil in a saucepan. Cook the dough squares in batches in the boiling water for 4-6 minutes or until al dente. When cooked, remove them carefully using a slotted spoon, and place them in a bowl of cold water to cool. (Shop-bought cannelloni should be filled uncooked.)
5. To make the béchamel sauce, melt the butter, add the flour and cook it until it is well blended. Stirring constantly with an egg whisk, gradually pour in the milk, and allow the sauce to thicken over a low heat, while stirring constantly. Season with salt and nutmeg.
6. Preheat the oven to 225°C/425°F/Gas Mark 7. Butter an ovenproof dish.
7. Arrange the well-drained cannelloni on a serving dish, place a generous amount of filling on one side of each square, then roll each square into a cylinder shape. In the case of cannelloni purchased from a shop, fill the rolls using a teaspoon or piping bag.
8. Arrange the cannelloni side by side in the ovenproof dish seam downwards.
9. Pour the béchamel sauce over the cannelloni, dot generously with butter, and sprinkle with Parmesan.
10. Bake on the centre shelf of the oven for 15-20 minutes or until golden brown. Serve in the dish.
Recommended wine:
a light red wine.

RAVIOLI WITH RICOTTA FILLING

SERVES 4 ■■
*Preparation and cooking
time: 1 hour
Kcal per portion: 885
P = 33g, F = 51g, C = 75g*

FOR THE DOUGH:
*400g/14oz strong plain flour
2 eggs
10 tbsps water*

FOR THE FILLING:
*300g/10oz spinach
30g/1oz butter
300g/10oz Ricotta
2 egg yolks
salt
freshly grated nutmeg
40g/1¹/₂oz freshly grated
   Parmesan*

Dot half of the dough with the spinach-ricotta filling; then cover it with the other half of the dough.

1. To make the dough, place the flour on a wooden board and make a well in the centre. Add the eggs and the water, and knead briskly by hand to make a smooth dough. Wrap in a damp cloth and leave to stand for 20 minutes.
2. To make the filling, wash the spinach, place in a pan with the rinsing water still clinging to it, and boil for a few minutes until soft. Then chop finely. Melt the butter in a pan, add the spinach and sauté for a few minutes. Leave to cool.
3. Combine the Ricotta and the egg yolks with the spinach, seasoning generously with salt and nutmeg. Then add the Parmesan.
4. Using either a pasta-making machine or a rolling pin, roll the dough out thinly. Place tiny dabs of filling on one half of the dough at 4-cm/¹/₂ inch intervals.
5. Place the other half of the dough on top, and using a pastry wheel, cut out small squares, pressing the edges of each square together firmly.

Cut out the squares using a pastry wheel.

6. Bring a generous quantity of salted water to the boil in a saucepan. Cook the ravioli in batches in the water for 5-7 minutes or until al dente. Remove with a slotted spoon and serve on 4 warmed plates.
7. Heat the butter in a pan, add the sage leaves and sauté them for a few minutes. Scatter them over the ravioli. Finally, sprinkle with the Parmesan.
Recommended wine:
a slightly sparkling Italian red wine, such as Lambrusco.

PIZZA WITH TOMATOES AND MOZZARELLA

SERVES 4: ■
*Preparation and cooking
time: 45 minutes
Rising time: 2 hours 15
minutes
Kcal per portion: 915
P = 38g, F = 41g, C = 94g*

FOR THE PIZZA DOUGH:
*500g/1lb 2oz strong plain
   flour
1 tsp salt
20g/³/₄oz fresh yeast
just under 250ml/8 fl oz
   lukewarm water
oil for greasing the baking
   sheet*

FOR THE TOPPING:
*500g/1lb 2oz very ripe
   tomatoes
or 1 can of tomatoes
   (400g/14oz)
8 anchovy fillets, soaked in
   water
300g/10oz Mozzarella
8 fresh basil leaves
salt
freshly ground black pepper
dried oregano
8 tbsps olive oil
4 tbsps freshly grated
   Parmesan*

1. For the dough, mix the flour and salt together in a bowl. Make a well in the centre, crumble in the yeast, add half the water and knead together some of the flour with the water and yeast to make a starter. Cover and leave to rise in a warm place for 15 minutes.
2. Knead with the remaining water to make a smooth dough that no longer sticks to the bowl. Cover and leave to rise in a warm place for 1 hour.
3. Divide the dough into 4 balls, then press each ball flat to make a round with a raised rim. Cover and leave to rise again for 1 hour.
4. To make the topping, blanch and skin the tomatoes, cut out the stalk bases and chop. If using canned tomatoes, drain well and crush. Chop the anchovies finely.
5. Preheat the oven to 250°C/475°F/Gas Mark 9. Oil the baking sheet.
6. Place the four dough rounds on the baking sheet. Top with the tomatoes and anchovies. Slice the Mozzarella and arrange it over the top. Season with the chopped basil leaves, salt, pepper and oregano. Sprinkle 2 tbsps olive oil over each pizza and garnish with Parmesan.
7. Place on the centre shelf of the oven and bake for 10 minutes. The pizza bases should not be allowed to brown. Serve immediately on heated plates.
Recommended wine: a full-bodied Italian red wine.

> **TIP**
>
> *In the nineteenth century, a pizza chef was asked to bake a special pizza in honour of Queen Margherita of Savoy. His creation reflected the colours of the Italian flag: red (tomatoes), white (mozzarella) and green (basil). Thus the Pizza Margherita was born!*

SEAFOOD PIZZA

SERVES 4 ■ ■

*Preparation and cooking
time: 1 hour
Rising time: 2 hours 15
minutes
Kcal per portion: 725
P = 19g, F = 29g, C = 93g*

FOR THE PIZZA DOUGH:
*500g/1lb 2oz strong plain
    flour
2 tsps salt
20g/³/₄oz fresh yeast
just under 250ml/8 fl oz
    lukewarm water
oil for the baking sheet*

FOR THE TOPPING:
*1 onion
1 garlic clove
10 tsps olive oil
2 large, ripe tomatoes
salt
freshly ground black pepper
400g/14oz cooked mixed
    seafood (mussels, prawns,
    calamari)
1 tbsp chopped fresh parsley
dried oregano*

*Arrange the topping on the pizzas
after baking them blind.*

1. To make the dough, mix
the flour and salt in a bowl
and make a well in the centre. Crumble the yeast into
the well, add half the water
and knead some of the flour
with the water and yeast to
make a starter. Cover with a
tea towel and leave to rise in
a warm place for 15 minutes.
2. Add the remaining water
and knead the whole mix-
ture to make a smooth
dough that no longer sticks
to the base of the bowl.
Cover and leave to rise in a
warm place for 1 hour.
3. Divide the dough into 4
balls. Press each ball flat to
form a rimmed circle. Cover
again with a cloth and leave
to rise again for 1 hour.
4. Preheat the oven to
250°C/475°F/Gas Mark 9.
Grease the baking sheet
with oil.
5. For the topping, peel the
onion, dice finely and fry
with the peeled garlic clove
in 2 tbsps oil until transparent. Blanch, peel and chop
the tomatoes. Add them to
the diced onion and cook
the mixture for 10 minutes.
Season with salt and pepper.
Then add the seafood, and
heat through, without allowing the mixture to boil.
6. Place the 4 dough circles
on the baking sheet and
bake them blind on the centre shelf of the oven for 10
minutes.
7. Remove the pizza bases
from the oven and spread
them with the seafood and
sauce. Sprinkle with the
parsley and oregano, then
sprinkle each pizza with 2
tbsps oil, and finish baking
on the centre shelf of the
oven for 1 minute. Serve
immediately.
Recommended wine:
Italian white wine, such
as Trebbiano (from the
Abruzzi).

PIZZA WITH TUNA AND SPINACH

SERVES 8 ■

*Preparation and cooking
time: 1 hour
Rising time: 2 hours 15
minutes
Kcal per portion: 825
P = 32g, F = 33g, C = 95g*

FOR THE PIZZA DOUGH:
*1kg/2¹/₄ lbs strong plain flour
2 tsps salt
40g/1¹/₂oz fresh yeast
just under 500ml/16 fl oz
    lukewarm water
oil for the baking sheet*

FOR THE TOPPING:
*1kg/2¹/₄ lbs spinach
salt
2 onions
10 tbsps olive oil
freshly ground black pepper
250g/8 oz canned tuna
large handful of parsley
12 fresh basil leaves,
    cut into strips
200g/7oz freshly grated
    Parmesan
100g/4oz chopped pine
    kernels*

1. For the dough, mix the
flour and salt in a bowl and
make a well in the centre.
Crumble the yeast into the
well, add half the water, and
knead some of the flour with
the yeast and water to make
a starter. Cover and leave to
rise in a warm place for 15
minutes.
2. Add the remaining water
and knead the mixture to
make a smooth dough that
no longer sticks to the bowl.
Cover and again leave to rise
in a warm place for 1 hour.
3. Shape the risen dough
into a rectangle and place it
on an oiled baking sheet.
Then press it flat until it cov-
ers the whole sheet, shaping
a rim around the edge.
Cover with a cloth and leave
to rise again for 1 hour.
4. Preheat the oven to
250°C/475°F/Gas Mark 9.

*Cover the dough with a cloth and
leave to rise on the baking sheet
for 1 hour. Then cover it with the
topping.*

5. To make the topping,
wash the spinach. Cook it
with the water still clinging
to it with a little salt for a few
minutes. Drain well and
chop finely. Peel and dice
the onions, then fry them in
4 tbsps oil until transparent.
Add the spinach, and season
with salt and pepper.
6. Spread the onion and
spinach mixture over the
dough. Cover it with
chopped tuna. Season with
finely chopped parsley, basil
leaves, salt and pepper. Top
with Parmesan and pine kernels and sprinkle with the
remaining oil.
7. Place the pizza on the
centre shelf of the oven and
bake for 20 minutes. Slice
before serving.
Recommended wine:
a dry Italian rosé.

RISOTTO WITH SCAMPI

SERVES 4 ■■

Preparation and cooking time: 1½ hours
Kcal per portion: 965
P = 36g, F = 31g, C = 125g

500g/1lb 2oz scampi or
   prawns
2 small onions
1 garlic clove
1 carrot
1 stick of celery
3 tbsps olive oil
1¼ l/2¼ pints water
salt
100g/4oz butter
400g/14oz Italian short-grain
   rice
125ml/4 fl oz white wine
100g/4oz mushrooms
2 tomatoes
300g/10oz young peas,
   shelled
25g/1oz butter (optional)

Fry the carrots, celery, onions and garlic with the unshelled scampi.

Crush the scampi shells finely using a pestle and mortar and add them to the stock.

1. Wash the scampi. Peel and dice the onions, peel the garlic clove and chop it finely. Clean the carrot and slice it into strips. Cut the celery into slices.
2. Heat the oil in a pan. Add half the diced onion, the garlic, the strips of carrot and sliced celery; sauté for 5 minutes. Then add the scampi and fry for a few more minutes. Add the boiling water and season with salt. Boil for 10 minutes, then drain in a colander, retaining the liquid.
3. Peel the scampi and set the flesh aside. Crush the shells finely, using a pestle and mortar and add them to the scampi stock.
4. Sauté the remaining diced onion in 50g/2oz butter. Then add the rice and, stirring frequently, fry until transparent. Strain the scampi stock and add the wine to it. Gradually pour it into the rice mixture. The rice should be kept boiling vigorously.
5. Clean and slice the mushrooms. Blanch, skin and chop the tomatoes.
6. Melt the remaining butter in a pan. Add the peas, mushrooms and chopped tomato and sauté for 10 minutes. Season with salt. Then add the scampi and cook for a further 3 minutes. Combine with the cooked rice. Butter may be added to make a richer dish.

Recommended wine:
a delicate, dry white wine.

ITALIAN TURNOVERS

SERVES 4 ■■

Preparation and cooking time: 45 minutes
Rising time: 2 hours 15 minutes
Kcal per portion: 1275
P = 53g, F = 71g, C = 93g

FOR THE DOUGH:
500g/1lb 2oz strong plain
   flour
1 tsp salt
30g/1oz fresh yeast
250ml/8 fl oz lukewarm
   water
60g/2oz lard

FOR THE FILLING:
200g/7oz Ricotta cheese
2 eggs
2 tbsps chopped fresh parsley
100g/4oz freshly grated
   Parmesan
450g/1 lb pepperoni
200g/7oz Mozzarella
freshly ground black pepper
oil for frying

1. To make the dough, mix the flour and salt in a bowl. Make a well in the centre and crumble in the yeast. Using a spoon, mix half the water with some of the flour and the yeast to make a starter. Cover and leave to rise in a warm place for about 15 minutes.
2. Add the remaining water and the melted lard, kneading until the mixture forms a smooth dough which no longer sticks to the bowl. Cover and leave to rise in a warm place for a further hour.
3. Once the dough has risen, divide it into 4 balls. Then, using a rolling pin, roll out each ball into a circle, forming a rim around the edge with your fingers. Cover with a cloth and leave to rise again for 1 hour.
4. To make the filling, whisk the eggs with the Ricotta, then add the parsley and Parmesan. Skin the sausages and dice them finely. Cut the

Cover one half of the dough with the cheese and sausage filling.

Fold the other half of the dough over the filling and press the edges together firmly.

Mozzarella into thin strips. Combine both with the Ricotta mixture. Season generously with pepper.
5. Spread the filling evenly over one side of each dough circle. Fold each of them in half, pressing the edges together firmly.
6. Heat a generous amount of oil in a deep pan. Fry the turnovers in the oil until golden-brown. Remove from the oil with a skimmer and drain on absorbent paper. The turnovers can also be baked on the centre shelf of a preheated oven for about 20 minutes.

Recommended wine:
Italian red table wine.

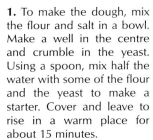

CHINESE STIR-FRIED NOODLES

SERVES 4 ■
*Preparation and cooking
time: 45 minutes
Kcal per portion: 45 minutes
P = 16g, F = 20g, C = 23g*

*150g/5¹/₂oz Chinese
    vermicelli
salt
100g/4oz chicken breast
100g/4oz pork fillet
2¹/₂ tsps cornflour
monosodium glutamate
    (optional)
1 tsp soy sauce
3 tbsps canned bamboo
    shoots
1 slice of cooked ham
5-6 tbsps peanut oil
100g/4oz broccoli florets
2 tbsps white wine
4 tbsps chicken stock*

1. Add the vermicelli to boiling salted water, separating any that stick together using a fork or 2 chopsticks. Boil for 2 minutes, then quickly transfer to a sieve, rinse with cold water and drain well. Leave to dry well on a plate or on a baking sheet lined with absorbent paper.
2. Cut the chicken and pork into thin strips, then combine it with ¹/₂ tsp cornflour, the soy sauce, and a generous pinch each of salt and monosodium glutamate, if used. Marinate the meat in the mixture for 15 minutes.
3. Drain the bamboo shoots and chop them coarsely. Slice the ham into strips and set it aside.
4. Heat 3 tbsps oil in a wok or wide pan. Add some of the vermicelli and stir-fry until golden brown. Remove them with a slotted spoon and drain. Repeat the same procedure with the next batch of vermicelli, stir-frying on both sides until golden-brown, adding more oil if necessary. Continue until all the vermicelli have been fried. Drain the oil remaining

in the wok and keep the vermicelli warm.
5. Heat another 2 tbsps oil in the wok, add the chicken, pork, and bamboo shoots, and fry until the meat is lightly browned. Then remove the mixture from the wok, add the broccoli florets and stir-fry them for 1 minute. Return the meat to the pan, season the mixture with salt and monosodium glutamate, if using, and heat through for a few minutes.
6. Combine the remaining cornflour, white wine and chicken stock to make a smooth sauce. Pour the sauce over the meat and vegetables. Boil the mixture, stirring frequently, until the ingredients are coated in sauce.
7. Place the noodles on a round serving dish with the meat and vegetable mixture in the centre and the strips of ham arranged on top. Serve immediately.
Recommended drink:
beer or China tea.

> ### TIP
> *Chinese noodles and vermicelli are generally sold in bundles: one bundle serves one person. Bean threads do not require pre-cooking, and are placed straight in the hot oil.*

CHINESE EGG NOODLES WITH GINGER AND SPRING ONIONS

SERVES 4 ■
*Preparation and cooking
time: 15 minutes
Kcal per portion: 410
P = 11g, F = 13g, C = 61g*

*400g/14oz fresh or 300g/
    10oz dried Chinese egg
    noodles
2 x 5cm/2 inch pieces of fresh
    ginger root
16 spring onions
4 tbsps peanut oil or corn oil
1 tsp salt
4 tbsps Chinese oyster sauce*

1. Bring a generous quantity of water to the boil in a large pan and add the noodles. Cook fresh noodles for 1-1¹/₂ minutes, and dried noodles for 4 minutes. Drain in a sieve, place in a serving dish and keep warm.
2. Peel the ginger root and cut it into thin strips. Clean the spring onions and slice them lengthways, also into thin strips, including the green ends.
3. Place a wok or sauté pan over a high heat. Add the oil and the strips of ginger and stir-fry for a few seconds. Then add the spring onions and continue stir-frying until the whole mixture is hot. Season with salt and remove the wok from the heat.
4. Place the egg noodles in the wok and stir thoroughly using a fork or two chopsticks. Add the oyster sauce and continue stirring. Serve on a preheated dish.
Recommended drink:
beer or China tea.

INDIAN LEMON RICE

Photo, page 38/39

SERVES 4 ■
*Preparation and cooking
time: 20 minutes
Kcal per portion: 405
P = 7g, F = 17g, C = 54g*

*250g/8oz long-grain rice
2l/3¹/₂ pints water
¹/₂ tsp salt
4 tbsps oil
1 tsp black mustard seeds
1 tsp turmeric
4 tbsps chopped cashew nuts
2 tbsps chopped peanuts
juice of 1 lemon
2 tbsps chopped fresh
    coriander leaves*

1. Place the rice in a sieve and wash under running water.
2. Add the salt to the water and bring it to the boil in a saucepan. Add the rice and cook for 12 minutes. Test the rice to see if it is al dente, and, if necessary, cook for a further 3 minutes. Then pour it into a sieve, rinse with cold water and drain well.
3. Heat the oil in a pan, add the mustard seeds, turmeric and chopped nuts and fry them for a few minutes. Then add the rice and stir-fry.
4. Remove the pan from the heat and mix the rice with the lemon juice. Place on a serving dish, using two forks to make a pyramid shape. Garnish with the coriander leaves.
Recommended drinks:
fruit juice or Planter's Punch.

INDONESIAN RICE

SERVES 4 ■

*Preparation and cooking
time: 1 hour
Kcal per portion: 575
P = 30g, F = 25g, C = 52g*

250g/8oz long-grain rice
salt
200g/7oz lean fillet of pork
200g/7oz chicken breast
1 leek
1 red pepper
2 onions
1 garlic clove
6 tbsps oil
freshly ground black pepper
½ tsp monosodium
   glutamate (optional)
150g/5½oz shrimps or
   prawns
2 eggs

**Fry the meat, shellfish and
vegetables one after the other in
the wok.**

**After frying, cut the omelette into
thin strips.**

1. Cook the rice in salted water for 12 minutes until al dente, then pour into a sieve, drain well and leave to dry out a little on a serving dish.
2. Slice the pork and chicken into strips. Seed the pepper and peel the onions; then slice the pepper, onions and the leek into strips. Peel the garlic clove and chop finely.

> ### TIP
> *Hard-boiled eggs,
> other types of
> vegetables and
> mushrooms may
> be added
> to the rice*

3. Heat 2 tbsps oil in a wok or sauté pan, add the meat and stir-fry until golden brown. Season with salt, pepper and, if wanted monosodium glutamate. Finally add the shellfish and heat through briefly before removing the mixture from the pan.
4. Heat a further 3 tbsps oil in the wok or pan, add the strips of onion and diced garlic, and fry them until transparent. Add the leek and pepper strips and stir-fry for a few minutes; the vegetables should still be crispy. Season with salt and pepper.
5. Whisk the eggs with a pinch of salt until they are frothy. Heat the remaining oil in a pan, pour in the egg and cook it to make a thin, yellow omelette.
6. Add the rice to the vegetables in the wok and stir-fry for a few minutes. Then add the meat, continue stir-frying until cooked, and season to taste.
7. Cut the omelette into thin strips.
8. Place the rice mixture in a serving dish and garnish with the strips of omelette.
Accompaniments: sambal oelek, roasted peanuts and ginger in syrup.
Recommended drinks: beer or rice wine.

GREEK MEAT PIE WITH OLIVES

SERVES 4-6 ■ ■

*Preparation and cooking
time: 1 hour 30 minutes
Kcal per portion, to serve 4:
2150
P = 65g, F = 153g, C = 108g*

900g/2lb frozen puff pastry
250g/8oz minced pork
3 onions
1 garlic clove
500g/1lb 2oz lean, finely
   minced beef
salt
freshly ground black pepper
3 eggs
125ml/5 fl oz double cream
150g/5½oz white bread-
   crumbs soaked in milk
10 anchovies, soaked in
   water
generous pinch each of
   oregano, thyme and
   cinnamon
100g/4oz pine kernels
150g/5½oz black olives
200g/7oz Feta cheese, finely
   diced
1-2 egg yolks, mixed with
   2 tsps water for glazing

**Decorate the top with pastry
strips and brush egg yolk over the
whole of the pastry lid.**

1. Allow the puff pastry to thaw for 20 minutes.
2. Peel the onions and the garlic clove, and combine with the minced pork in a food processor. Add the minced beef and mix well. Season with salt and pepper.

> ### TIP
> *This tempting bake
> is not for those
> following a diet!
> The extremely
> high calorie count
> is due mainly to
> the puff pastry
> and minced pork
> contained in
> the filling.*

3. Whisk the eggs with the cream. Drain some of the liquid from the breadcrumbs and chop the anchovies finely. Combine the eggs and cream, the breadcrumbs and anchovies with the minced meat, the herbs and spices. Finally stir in the chopped pine kernels, the olives and the Feta cheese.
4. Preheat the oven to 225°C/425°F/Gas Mark 7. Rinse a baking sheet with cold water.
5. Divide the dough in half and roll out each piece until it is a little larger than the baking sheet. Line the base and edges of the baking sheet with one sheet of dough. Distribute the meat filling evenly over the top and cover with the other sheet of dough, pressing the edges together firmly. Decorate with the remaining strips of dough and brush the pastry with egg yolk.
6. Place the baking sheet on the centre shelf of the oven and bake for 40 minutes or until golden brown.
7. Remove the pie from the oven and cut into quarters.
Recommended drink: Retsina.

BEEF FRIED RICE

SERVES 4 ■
*Preparation and cooking
time: 45 minutes
Standing time: 4 hours
Kcal per portion: 465
P = 19g, F = 18g, C = 50g*

*250g/8oz long-grain rice
salt
5 tbsps corn oil or peanut oil
250g/8oz lean steak
½ tsp sugar
2 tbsps soy sauce
freshly ground black pepper
2 tbsps dry sherry
1 tsp cornflour
4 garlic cloves
1 x 5-6cm/2-2¼ inch piece of
    ginger root
4 spring onions
1 egg
3 Chinese leaves or iceberg
    lettuce leaves*

1. Wash the rice, then cook in 500ml/16 fl oz salted water containing 1 tbsp oil for 12-15 minutes until soft, but al dente. Place in a dish and separate the grains using two forks. Leave to dry for 4 hours.
2. Chop the meat very finely or mince it. Place it in a bowl.
3. Add ½ tsp salt, the sugar, soy sauce, pepper, 1 tbsp sherry, 4 tbsps water and the cornflour to the bowl and stir thoroughly into the meat. Stir the mixture with a small egg whisk until the meat is light and fluffy. Then leave to stand for 15 minutes. Finally add 1 tbsp oil.
4. Peel the garlic cloves and the ginger. Chop both finely. Slice the spring onions into rings, separating the green and white sections.
5. Heat the remaining oil in a wok. Add first the garlic and then the ginger and white spring onion rings, stir-frying for a few minutes. Then add the meat and continue frying, stirring with a wooden spatula. Do not allow the meat to form lumps. Pour the rest of the sherry over it.

Stir-fry the meat in the wok.

6. Beat the egg lightly and pour it over the meat mixture. Then add the rice and mix the ingredients together.
7. Cut the lettuce or Chinese cabbage leaves into very fine strips. Stir half of the leaves and the green onion rings into the fried rice. Serve garnished with the remaining strips of lettuce or cabbage.

Recommended drink: beer or China tea.

> **TIP**
>
> *The wok is the most important cooking utensil in China: finely chopped ingredients (vegetables, meat or fish) are stir-fried briefly over a high heat so that they stay crispy and nutritious.*

INDIAN VEGETABLE RICE

SERVES 4 ■
*Preparation and cooking
time: 1 hour
Kcal per portion: 315
P = 7g, F = 6g, C = 57g*

*250g/8oz basmati rice
3 firm tomatoes
1 x 6cm/2¼ inch piece of
    ginger root
6 black peppercorns
250ml/8 fl oz water or
    unsalted vegetable stock
1 large onion
1 garlic clove
2 tbsps clarified butter or
    vegetable ghee
1 cinnamon stick
6 cloves
2 large black or 4 large green
    cardamon pods, lightly
    crushed
1 bay leaf
½ tsp turmeric
1 tsp salt
600g/1lb 6oz mixed fresh
    vegetables (such as green
    beans, peas, carrots,
    cauliflower florets)
lemon slices for garnishing*

1. Wash the rice thoroughly, soak for 20 minutes and then drain.
2. Cut the tomatoes into quarters. Peel the ginger root and grate it finely. Place the quartered tomatoes, the peppercorns, water or stock and ginger in a small saucepan and bring the mixture to the boil. Reduce the heat, cover the pan and boil for 10-12 minutes. Then rub the mixture through a sieve and add sufficient water to make 500ml/16 fl oz tomato stock. Set the liquid aside.
3. Peel the onion and garlic clove and chop finely.
4. Heat the fat in a pan over a medium heat. Add the onion, garlic, cinnamon stick, cloves, cardamon and bay leaf, and fry for a few seconds. Add the rice and continue stir-frying for about 2 minutes.
5. Add the tomato stock, the

turmeric and salt and bring the mixture to the boil. Reduce the heat immediately, cover the pan with a tight-fitting lid and cook the rice gently for 20-25 minutes until it is fluffy and all the liquid has been absorbed.
6. Meanwhile, clean the vegetables. Chop the beans, shell the peas and slice the carrots into julienne strips. Then cook the beans, peas, carrot and cauliflower florets in lightly salted water for a few minutes; the vegetables should remain crispy. Drain them in a sieve.
7. Remove the rice from the heat and scatter the vegetables on top of the rice. Replace the lid immediately and leave to stand for 5 minutes for the tender rice grains to become firm. Remove the lid, loosen the rice and stir in the vegetables. Transfer to a hot dish and garnish with a couple of lemon slices.

Accompaniments: fried bananas and sliced cucumber in a yoghurt dressing.
Recommended drink: mineral water or Indian tea.

> **TIP**
>
> *Basmati rice should be washed thoroughly before cooking to remove all particles of starch on the outside. It should then be covered with water and left to stand for 20-30 minutes before cooking.*

MOROCCAN MEAT COUSCOUS

SERVES 6 ■■

Preparation and cooking time: 2 hours 30 minutes
Soaking time: about 8 hours
Kcal per portion: 1085
P = 35g, F = 72g, C = 71g

50g/2oz chick-peas
2 onions
2 parsnips
2 large carrots
1kg/2¼ lb neck of lamb or 500g/1lb 2oz lamb,
250g/8oz beef and half a chicken
2 tbsps olive oil
salt
freshly ground black pepper
¼ tsp ground ginger
¼ tsp saffron strands
500g/1lb 2oz couscous
2 tomatoes
3 courgettes
50-100g/2-4oz raisins
100g/4oz fresh or frozen broad beans
4 tbsps finely chopped fresh parsley
cayenne pepper or chilli powder
1 tsp paprika
30g/1oz butter, cut into pieces

1. Soak the chick-peas for about 8 hours or overnight.
2. Peel the onions, parsnips and carrots. Dice the onion, cut the parsnips into quarters and slice the carrots.
3. Place the meat, onions, chick-peas, carrot and parsnip in the lower section of a couscousier. Cover with water, then add oil, salt, pepper, ginger and saffron. Cook gently for about 1 hour over a medium heat.
4. Dampen the couscous with a little cold water, mixing well using your fingers so that no lumps form.
5. When the meat is almost cooked, place the couscous in the top part of the couscousier and cook it over the meat for about 30 minutes. Loosen the grains from time to time with your

Soak the chick-peas overnight. Cook the meat with the carrot, parsnip and onion.

Place the couscous in a metal sieve over the saucepan.

After steaming for about 30 minutes over the stock, the couscous will have swollen.

fingers or a fork to help them swell up as they cook.
6. Place the couscous in a large bowl, pour over a generous quantity of cold water and stir with a wooden spoon in order to separate the grains and expose them to the air. Season to taste with salt.
7. Blanch and peel the tomatoes and cut them into quarters. Slice the courgettes. Add the tomatoes, courgettes, raisins, broad beans

and parsley to the meat stew.
8. Place the sieve containing the couscous over the stew for a further half hour.
9. Remove a cup of meat stock from the pan, stir in a little cayenne pepper and paprika to make it taste hot and spicy.

TIP

A couscousier is a tall two-part steamer with a lid. If you do not have one, use a vegetable steamer lined with muslin over a large, deep saucepan or stockpot. The peppery sauce can be made with harissa, a spicy tomato sauce .

10. Place the couscous on a large serving dish, preferably earthenware. Dot it with the butter so that it melts into the couscous. Cut the meat into large chunks and serve with the vegetables on top of the couscous. Pour the stock over it. Serve the hot, peppery sauce separately in a small bowl.
Recommended drinks:
mint tea or Algerian red wine.

TURKISH PILAF

SERVES 4 ■

Preparation and cooking time: 30 minutes
Kcal per portion: 490
P = 9g, F = 23g, C = 60g

250g/8oz long-grain rice
1 onion
60g/2oz butter
60g/2oz pine kernels
750ml/1¼ pints meat stock
few strands of saffron
60g/2oz currants
generous pinch of ground coriander
¼ tsp fennel seeds
¼ tsp salt
¼ tsp freshly-ground black pepper

1. Place the rice in a sieve and pour boiling water over it.
2. Peel and dice the onion and fry it in the butter until transparent. Add the rice and pine kernels, stir-frying the mixture for a few minutes. Then pour the meat stock over it and add the saffron. Finally, stir the currants, coriander, fennel, salt and pepper into the rice.
3. Cover the pan with a cloth and cook the pilaf over a low heat for 20-25 minutes.
Serve as an accompaniment to lamb or chicken curry.

QUICHE LORRAINE

SERVES 4-6 ■
Preparation and cooking time: 1 hour
Standing time: 2 hours
Kcal per portion, to serve 4: 1260
P = 15g, F = 107g, C = 48g

FOR THE DOUGH:
250g/8oz strong plain flour
½ tsp salt
125g/5oz butter, cut into pieces
4 tbsps ice-cold water
butter for the quiche dish
flour for the work surface

FOR THE FILLING:
250g/8oz smoked streaky bacon
15g/½oz butter
250ml/8 fl oz single cream
3 eggs
¼ tsp salt
½ tsp freshly ground black pepper
¼ tsp freshly grated nutmeg

1. To make the dough, place the flour in a bowl and make a well in the centre. Add the knobs of butter, plus the water, and knead the mixture briskly to make a smooth dough. Shape into a ball, wrap in clingfilm and refrigerate for 2 hours.

Spread the fried bacon over the quiche base and pour the cream-and-egg mixture over it.

225°C/425°F/Gas Mark 7. Butter a 24cm/9½ inch quiche dish.
4. Roll the dough out on a floured board until it is a little larger than the quiche dish. Line the base and sides of the dish with the dough, and arrange the bacon over it.
5. Whisk the egg and cream together, seasoning with salt, pepper and nutmeg. Pour the mixture over the bacon.
6. Bake the quiche on the centre shelf of the oven for 30-40 minutes or until golden brown. Then leave to cool on a wire rack for 20 minutes. Serve while still warm.
Recommended wine:
a light, fresh Silvaner or dry Riesling from Alsace.

> ### TIP
> *True Quiche Lorraine is made without cheese. The bacon is simply topped with a savoury custard. In the Loire valley, quiche is filled with pork rillettes.*

2. To make the filling, cut the bacon into thin strips. Heat the butter in a pan, add the bacon and fry until transparent. Leave to cool.
3. Preheat the oven to

QUICHE WITH SMOKED FISH

SERVES 4-6 ■
Preparation and cooking time: 1 hour 15 minutes
Standing time: 2 hours
Kcal per portion, to serve 4: 780
P = 17g, F = 55g, C = 49g

FOR THE DOUGH:
250g/8oz strong plain flour
½ tsp salt
125g/5oz butter, cut into pieces
4 tbsps ice-cold water

FOR THE FILLING:
150g/5½oz smoked fish
125ml/4 fl oz milk
salt
3 eggs
125ml/5 fl oz single cream
freshly ground black pepper
freshly-grated nutmeg

PLUS:
butter for the quiche dish
flour for the work surface
40g/1½ oz butter, cut into pieces

1. To make the dough, mix the flour and salt in a bowl. Add the knobs of butter and the water. Knead briskly by hand to make a smooth dough. Shape the dough into a ball, wrap in clingfilm and refrigerate for 2 hours.
2. To make the filling, bring the smoked fish briefly to the boil in the milk and 125ml/4 fl oz water, then drain off the liquid and set it aside. Skin and bone the drained fish and flake it. Whisk together the eggs with the cream and 125ml/4 fl oz of the fish liquid, seasoning with salt, pepper and nutmeg.
3. Preheat the oven to 200°C/400°F/Gas Mark 6. Grease a 24cm/9½ inch quiche dish or springform tin.
4. Roll the dough out on a floured board until it is a little larger than the oven dish. Line the base and sides of

The smoked fish and egg-and-cream mixture are dotted with butter before baking.

the dish neatly with the dough. Arrange the pieces of fish in it, then pour the egg and cream mixture over it. Dot with butter. Place the quiche on the centre shelf of the oven and bake for 30-40 minutes or until golden brown. Allow to cool a little before serving.
Accompaniment:
mixed salad greens.
Recommended wine:
a dry white wine, such as Entre-deux-mers.

> ### TIP
> *Salmon makes this a gourmet dish. Sliced smoked or pickled salmon is divided into pieces, laid on the quiche dough and baked in the egg and cream mixture.*

Special Occasion Recipes

Culinary excursions to the regions of Italy provide proof that Italian dishes such as pasta and pizza are capable of satisfying the standards of even the most demanding gourmet, as is also demonstrated by the offerings of the best Italian restaurants over here. Skilled preparation and first-class ingredients can transform a simple pasta dish into a veritable feast. Spaghetti with chicken and fresh mushrooms, bucatoni with tender green peas, turkey fillet and cheese sauce are all original creations from the modern Italian kitchen. Unusual ingredients such as millet, cracked wheat, bulgar wheat and wild rice also have their place in gourmet cuisine. Examples of such dishes include millet risotto with chicken livers and basil, gnocchi made with bulgar wheat and served with fresh tomato sauce, or wild rice with grapes and quail.

Pasta with Asparagus and Salmon (see recipe on page 60)

PASTA WITH ASPARAGUS AND SALMON

Photo, page 58/59

SERVES 4 ■

*Preparation and cooking
time: 45-50 minutes
Kcal per portion: 560
P = 24g, F = 29g, C = 45g*

15g/½ oz butter
1 sugar cube
500g/1lb 2oz asparagus
200ml/7 fl oz single cream
salt
freshly ground white pepper
250g/8oz home-made pasta
250g/8oz fresh salmon, boned
small handful of chervil

1. Place 10g/¼oz butter and the sugar cube in 1l/1¾ pints boiling salted water. Tie the asparagus together and cook in the water, with the tips facing upwards, for 20-30 minutes.
2. Cut off the asparagus tips (about 8cm/3inches in length) and place them in the cooking water to keep warm. Chop 4 of the asparagus stems finely and purée in a blender with 2 tbsps of the cooking water. Place the purée with the cream in a frying pan and boil until a light, creamy sauce is formed. Season with salt and pepper.
3. Cook the pasta in a generous quantity of water until al dente.
4. Cut the salmon into small pieces. Use the rest of the butter to coat a vegetable steamer and place the pieces of fish in the steamer. Fill a suitable saucepan with water to a depth of 3cm/1¼ inches, place the steamer in the pan and steam the salmon for 1-2 minutes.
5. Mix the pasta with the salmon and sauce. Garnish with the asparagus tips. Wash the chervil, chop finely with scissors and use to garnish.

Cut the tips (about 8cm/3 inches) off the cooked asparagus and place them in the cooking water to keep warm.

Chop four of the asparagus stems finely and purée in a blender with some of the cooking water.

Butter a vegetable steamer.

Cook the diced salmon in the steamer.

SEAFOOD TAGLIATELLE

SERVES 4 ■ ■ ■

*Preparation and cooking
time: 50 minutes
Kcal per portion: 565
P = 12g, F = 22g, C = 47g*

250g/8oz mange-tout or baby
   green beans
250g/8oz home-made
   tagliatelle (preferably
   green)
2 tbsps finely chopped
   shallots
2 tbsps finely chopped leek
half a glass of white wine
250g/8oz mixed shellfish
   (such as scallops, crayfish,
   shrimps, prawns or cockles)
500ml/16 fl oz white wine
   vinegar
80g/3oz butter
2-3 tbsps cream
salt
½ tsp coarsely ground
   white pepper

1. Top and tail the mange-tout and trim the beans. Cook in 1l/1¾ pints boiling salted water for 5-10 minutes. Drain and rinse in cold water. Cook the pasta in a generous amount of boiling water until al dente.

TIP

*The butter should
be very cold when
added to the
sauce, so that it
combines slowly
with the liquid.
If the butter does
not thicken the
liquid, a little
cream should
be added.*

2. Boil the shallots and leek in the white wine for 10 minutes. Shell and clean the shellfish and, depending on their size, cook for between 3 and 5 minutes in the wine, leaving them in the liquid to keep warm.
3. Reserve some of the seafood, leaving it whole for garnishing. Chop the remainder finely. Mix the pasta with the chopped seafood.
4. Strain the wine sauce through a sieve into a frying pan. Add the vinegar and boil until the liquid is reduced by half. Cut the butter into small pieces and stir it into the simmering sauce using an egg whisk. Then add the cream and season with salt and pepper.
5. Drain the pasta and toss it with the seafood and vegetables. Pour the sauce over the top and garnish with the reserved seafood.
Recommended wine:
Chardonnay or a white Burgundy.

This recipe uses the best seafood: scallops, scampi, crayfish and prawns.

Mange-tout always need topping, tailing and stringing, unlike baby green beans.

BEEF AND MUSHROOM CHOP SUEY

SERVES 4   ■ ■

Preparation and cooking time: 40 minutes
Kcal per portion: 545
P = 30g, F = 13g, C = 70g

10g/^{1}/$_4$ oz Chinese cloud-ear
   mushrooms
1 tsp salt
250g/8oz lean beef
300g/10oz mixed vegetables
   (such as carrots, celery,
   leek, broccoli)
100g/4oz bean sprouts,
   drained
2 tbsps peanut oil
1 tbsp very finely chopped
   ginger root
2 garlic cloves
400g/14oz Chinese noodles

FOR THE SAUCE:
250ml/8 fl oz chicken stock
1 tsp cornflour
2 tbsps sake (rice wine) or
   dry sherry
2 tbsps soy sauce
^{1}/$_4$ tsp sambal oelek

1. Place the mushrooms in a small bowl and cover them with water. Bring 4l/7 pints salted water to the boil. Add

Slice the beef thinly.

All the vegetables are likewise sliced finely; the broccoli is divided into small florets.

> **TIP**
>
> *Do not use more than 10g/^{1}/$_4$oz mushrooms, since they swell considerably when soaked and are very rich.*

the noodles and cook them until they are al dente.
2. Cut the meat into small, thin slices. Clean the vegetables and cut them into strips. Place the bean sprouts in a sieve and blanch them with boiling water.
3. Heat 1 tbsp oil in a large pan or wok. Place the meat in the pan and stir-fry briefly over a high heat. Then

remove the slices and set them aside.
4. Heat the remaining oil in the pan. Add the vegetables, the bean sprouts, the mushrooms, ginger root, crushed garlic and a generous pinch of salt; stir-fry without allowing the vegetables to lose their crispness. Remove the mixture from the pan and combine it with the meat.
5. To make the sauce, combine all the sauce ingredients thoroughly. Place them in the pan or wok and heat, stirring constantly, until the sauce begins to thicken. Season to taste. Stir the meat and vegetables into the hot sauce. Heat the mixture through briefly, but do not allow it to boil.
6. Drain the noodles, place them on a serving dish and top with the meat sauce.
Recommended drinks: beer, rosé wine or tea.

SPAGHETTI WITH VEAL AND MUSHROOMS

SERVES 4   ■ ■

Preparation and cooking time: 40 minutes
Kcal per portion: 855
P = 41g, F = 37g, C = 81g

400g/14oz tomatoes
200g/7oz small mushrooms
salt
400-500g/14oz-1lb 2oz
   spaghetti
400g/14oz cooked veal,
   shredded
1^1/$_2$ tbsps olive oil
1 onion,
   chopped
1 garlic clove, peeled and
   crushed
freshly ground black pepper
^{1}/$_2$ tsp chopped fresh oregano
250ml/8 fl oz double cream
40g/1^1/$_2$oz freshly grated
   Parmesan
2 tbsps chopped fresh parsley

1. Blanch the tomatoes in boiling water, then skin, seed and dice them. Clean, wash and slice the mushrooms. Combine the mushrooms with the tomatoes.
2. Bring 2l/3^1/$_2$ pints salted water to the boil. Add the

It is easy to skin tomatoes if they are first dipped in very hot water.

The quickest and easiest way to slice mushrooms is to use an egg-slicer.

> **TIP**
>
> *Oil is often added to the water when cooking pasta; this stops the pasta from sticking. However, if the pasta is cooked al dente, this is not necessary. Pasta should usually be cooked al dente, which means that it should still be firm to the bite. Cooking times for pasta vary enormously.*

spaghetti and immerse it thoroughly using a wooden spoon, ensuring that the strands do not stick together. Boil for about 10 minutes.
3. Heat the olive oil in a pan, add the meat and stir-fry for 3-4 minutes. Then remove it from the pan and add the onions, tomatoes, mushrooms and garlic. Sauté the vegetables for 5 minutes, seasoning with salt, pepper and oregano. Then add the cream and boil for a further 3 minutes to reduce the liquid. Return the meat to the pan and heat through gently, without allowing the mixture to boil.
4. Drain the spaghetti, grind pepper over it and immediately stir in the cheese. Top with the sauce and garnish with the parsley.
Recommended wine: Merlot or Chianti.

PIZZA WITH SARDINES

SERVES 4   ■■
*Preparation and cooking
time: 1 hour 10 minutes
Kcal per portion: 780
P = 28g, F = 39g, C = 73g*

500g/1lb 2oz pizza dough
olive oil for the baking sheet
300g/10oz sardines
salt
freshly ground black pepper
1 tsp chopped fresh oregano
1 small piece of red chilli
2 tbsps olive oil
2 onions
150g/5½oz Mozzarella
50g/2oz black olives

1. Divide the dough in half, shape into balls, press flat and roll out with a rolling pin into two 25cm/10 inch rounds. Place each on an oiled baking sheet, ensuring that each base has a slightly raised rim around the edge.
2. Preheat the oven to 260°C/500°F/Gas Mark 10.
3. Before gutting the sardines, scale them using the blunt edge of a knife or a special scaling implement. Cut off the heads, slit them open and remove the guts. Pull out the bones. Then arrange them in the shape of a star on the pizzas. Sprinkle over a little salt, pepper and oregano.
4. Blanch the tomatoes with hot water, and then skin, seed, and chop them finely. Sauté them gently for a few minutes with the chilli in 1 tsp olive oil, then arrange them evenly between the sardines. Peel the onions, slice them into rings, and place them on top of each pizza.
5. Slice the Mozzarella finely and arrange over the pizzas. Sprinkle with salt and pepper. Stone the olives, chop them finely and scatter them on top. Sprinkle both pizzas with the remaining olive oil.

Before gutting, scale the fish using a sharp knife.

To clean the sardines, cut off the heads, slit them open at the belly and gut them.

Arrange the sardines in a star pattern on the pizza and sprinkle with the herbs.

Bake the pizzas, one after the other if necessary, on the centre shelf of the oven for 10 minutes at 260°C/500°F/Gas Mark 10; then reduce the temperature to 240°C/475°F/Gas Mark 9 and cook for a further 15 minutes.
Recommended wine: Italian red wine.

CAMARGUE RICE RISOTTO WITH CALVES' KIDNEYS

SERVES 4   ■■
*Preparation and cooking
time: 1 hour 40 minutes
Soaking time for the rice:
12 hours
Kcal per portion: 560
P = 22g, F = 16g, C = 63g*

300g/10oz wholegrain red
   rice from the Camargue
1 large onion
2 garlic cloves
4 tbsps olive oil
1 small bay leaf
1 clove
400ml/12 fl oz red wine
   (Merlot or Barolo)
600ml/18 fl oz chicken stock
400g/14oz calves' kidneys
   (surrounded by a thin
   layer of fat)
1 tsp honey
salt
pepper
2 tbsps chopped curly-leaved
   parsley

1. The evening before, soak the rice in cold water. Chop the onion finely. Peel and crush the garlic.
2. Heat 2 tbsps olive oil. Add the drained rice and fry for 2-3 minutes over a high heat. then add the bay leaf and the clove. Pour the red wine over the rice. As soon as the wine has been reduced, slowly add the chicken stock, stirring frequently. Cook the rice for 70-80 minutes. When cooked, it should be soft, but firm to bite.
3. Place the kidneys in a heated frying pan, and stir-fry until they are golden brown; the fat will melt in the process. Remove them from the pan and place them in a sieve with a dish underneath to collect the fat. Set aside the dish containing the fat.
4. When the rice is cooked, cover the pan with a lid, leave it to rest for 2-3 minutes and then season with honey, salt and pepper.

Fry the calves' kidneys in a heated pan to melt the fat.

Cut the kidneys into slices about 7.5mm/¾ inch thick.

Fry the kidney slices on both sides in the kidney fat until crispy.

Discard the bay leaf and the clove.
5. Cut the kidneys into slices about 7.5mm/¼ inch thick. Fry briskly on both sides in the hot kidney fat.
6. Combine the garlic with the onion, parsley, oil, salt and pepper.
7. Place the rice in a serving dish, arrange the kidney slices on top and sprinkle over the parsley and garlic oil.
Accompaniment: broccoli.
Recommended wine: Chianti or Merlot.

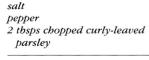

RISOTTO WITH CLAMS AND SCAMPI

SERVES 4 ■ ■ ■
Preparation and cooking time: 1 hour
Kcal per portion: 400
P = 11g, F = 11g, C = 52g

500g/1lb 2oz clams or cockles
4 tbsps olive oil
200ml/6 fl oz white wine
10 scampi, deveined, heads removed
60g/2oz diced celeriac
60g/2oz diced carrot
600g/2oz strips of leek
pinch of sugar
1 tbsp whisky or brandy
just over 500ml/16 fl oz chicken stock
salt
freshly ground white pepper
3 shallots, chopped
1 garlic clove
240g/8oz risotto rice
50g/2 oz curly-leaved parsley

1. Wash the clams. Heat 1 tbsp olive oil, add the clams and fry for a few minutes. Add the white wine and bring it to the boil. Then pour the clams into a sieve, reserving the cooking liquid.
2. Shell the scampi, reserving four of them.

When cooked in liquid, shellfish should open up. It is important to discard any that remain closed.

seasoning with salt and pepper. Boil the scampi cooking liquid for 30 minutes (or 10 minutes if using a pressure cooker), then strain it through a sieve.
4. To make the risotto, heat the remaining olive oil, add the rice and fry until shiny. Peel and crush the garlic, then add it to the pan, together with the shallots. Strain the clam juice and pour it over the rice. Boil until the liquid has reduced a little, then top it up gradually with the scampi cooking liquid. Cook the rice for 15-18 minutes until al dente, stirring occasionally.
5. Shell all but 12 of the clams and heat them in the risotto along with 6 finely chopped scampi. Season with salt and pepper.
6. Serve the risotto on 4 plates, garnishing each with 3 unshelled clams, 1 scampi and a little parsley.
Recommended wine:
Italian white wine, such as Soave, Verdicchio, Pinot grigio (Friuli).

> **TIP**
>
> *For this recipe, frozen headless scampi may be used; they should be thawed in the refrigerator before peeling. If fresh clams are not available, preserved or frozen clams can be used.*

3. Sauté the celeriac, carrot, leek and scampi shells lightly in 1 tbsp olive oil. Add the sugar and whisky or brandy. Top up with the stock,

WILD RICE WITH GRAPES AND QUAIL

SERVES 4 ■ ■
(as an hors d'oeuvre)
Preparation and cooking time: 1 hour 10 minutes
Kcal per portion: 380
P = 17g, F = 15g, C = 37g

2 dressed quails
salt
freshly ground white pepper
30g/1oz clarified butter
3 tbsps chopped shallots
100ml/3 fl oz dry white wine
1l/1¾ pints chicken stock
2 sprigs of oregano
160g/5¾oz wild rice
½ tsp fresh oregano, finely chopped
150g/5½oz white grapes
20g/¾oz butter

1. Cut the quails in half, and rub them with salt and pepper. Melt the clarified butter and fry the birds on both sides until lightly browned; then place them on a wire rack or trivet.
2. Add the shallots to the clarified butter in the pan, and fry for 1-2 minutes. Add the white wine and boil briefly. Then add the chicken stock and the sprigs of oregano. Bring to the boil, strain the liquid through a sieve and return to the pan.

> **TIP**
>
> *The rice may also be garnished with pieces of chicken or veal sweetbreads. Pecan rice can be used instead of wild rice.*

3. Add the rice to the sauce and cook over a low heat for 30-35 minutes. Season with salt, pepper and oregano. Half-fill a pan with water and bring it to the boil. Place the rice in a suitable steamer in

The quails must be cut in half using a sharp knife.

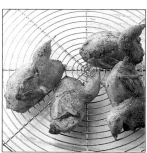
It is best to cool the fried quails on a wire rack.

Wild rice cooks over a low heat in about 30-35 minutes.

the pan, cover and finish cooking over the steam for 10-15 minutes.
4. Peel the grapes, cut them in half, remove the pips and warm the grapes slightly in the melted butter. Stir into the rice and serve on preheated plates. Place half a quail on top of each.
Recommended wine:
Chasselas or Cabernet-Sauvignon.

POLENTA WITH SAVOY CABBAGE

SERVES 4   ■
*Preparation and cooking
time: 50 minutes
Kcal per portion: 590
P = 26g, F = 27g, C = 55g*

2 tbsps olive oil
1½l/2½ pints meat stock
250g/8oz coarse cornmeal
salt
freshly ground white pepper
200g/7oz cooked pork,
   shredded
50g/2oz smoked streaky
   bacon
1 large onion, chopped
2 tbsps meat stock
2 tbsps chopped fresh herbs
   (parsley, marjoram, chervil)
1 medium-sized Savoy
   cabbage (500g/1lb 2oz)
3 tbsps freshly-grated
   Gruyère cheese

*Polenta is made from either
coarse or fine cornmeal.*

*The stem should be cut out from
each individual cabbage leaf.*

1. Oil a shallow ovenproof
dish.
2. Bring the meat stock to
the boil and stir in the cornmeal. Cook over a low heat

> **TIP**
>
> *Turkey or mixed
> minced meat may
> also be used with
> this recipe. The
> Savoy cabbage
> can be replaced
> by Chinese leaves,
> which should be
> blanched for a
> minute or two in
> salted water. The
> dish can be made
> more substantial
> by topping it with
> a Mornay sauce
> (white sauce
> mixed with
> grated cheese)
> instead of just
> cheese.*

for 40 minutes, stirring occasionally. Season with salt and
pepper.
3. Heat the remaining olive
oil in a pan, add the meat,
bacon and onion and fry for
a few minutes. Pour in 2
tbsps meat stock and season
with salt, pepper and the
herbs. Stir the meat into the
warm polenta.
4. Remove the Savoy cabbage leaves from their stalks.
Cut out the stems from the
individual leaves and blanch
the leaves for a few minutes
in boiling salted water.
Then remove and drain
thoroughly.
5. Line the ovenproof dish
with the leaves. Cover with
half the polenta, spreading it
out smoothly, then add
another layer of cabbage.
Finally, distribute the rest of
the polenta on top. Sprinkle
with the cheese.
6. Place the dish under the
grill and heat the polenta
until the cheese melts.
Accompaniment: tomato
salad.
Recommended drink:
Valpolicella or Merlot.

MILLET RISOTTO WITH CHICKEN LIVERS AND BASIL

SERVES 4   ■ ■
*Preparation and cooking
time: 45 minutes
Kcal per portion: 370
P = 21g, F = 14g, C = 32g*

FOR THE MILLET RISOTTO:
15g/½ oz butter
1 large onion, finely chopped
200g/7oz millet
125ml/4 fl oz white wine
500ml/16 fl oz vegetable stock
salt
freshly ground white pepper

250g/8oz chicken livers
15g/½ oz clarified butter
20g/¾ oz butter
1 large onion, finely chopped
8 fresh basil leaves
salt
freshly ground white pepper

*Fry the millet gently in the butter
before adding liquid.*

*Clean the chicken livers, trim
them; then cut into slices.*

1. To make the risotto, heat
the butter in a pan, add the
onion and sauté over a medium heat until transparent.
Then add the millet and stir,
still over the heat, until all the
grains are coated in the butter. Pour over the white wine
and just under half of the
vegetable stock, bringing the

> **TIP**
>
> *Millet is very
> flavoursome and
> cooks faster than
> any other grain.
> It is available
> from health food
> stores. The pan
> must be covered
> tightly during
> cooking so that
> the grain can
> swell. Strips of
> vegetable may be
> stirred into the
> risotto about 8
> minutes before
> the end of the
> cooking time.*

mixture to the boil. Cover
the pan with a tight-fitting lid
and cook over a low heat for
35 minutes, occasionally
adding a little more veg-
etable stock.
2. Trim the fat and impurities
from the chicken livers, then
slice them. Heat the clarified
butter, add the livers and fry
until browned. Remove
them from the pan and keep
them warm.
3. Heat the butter in the pan,
add the onions and fry them
for 2-3 minutes over a low
heat. Cut the basil leaves
into thin strips and combine
them with the onions.
Remove the pan from the
heat and stir in the liver.
Season with salt and pepper.
4. Add more seasoning to
the millet, if desired, then
place it on a serving dish and
arrange the livers in a shallow depression in the centre.
Accompaniment:
small tomato halves sautéed
in butter.
Recommended wine:
white table wine.

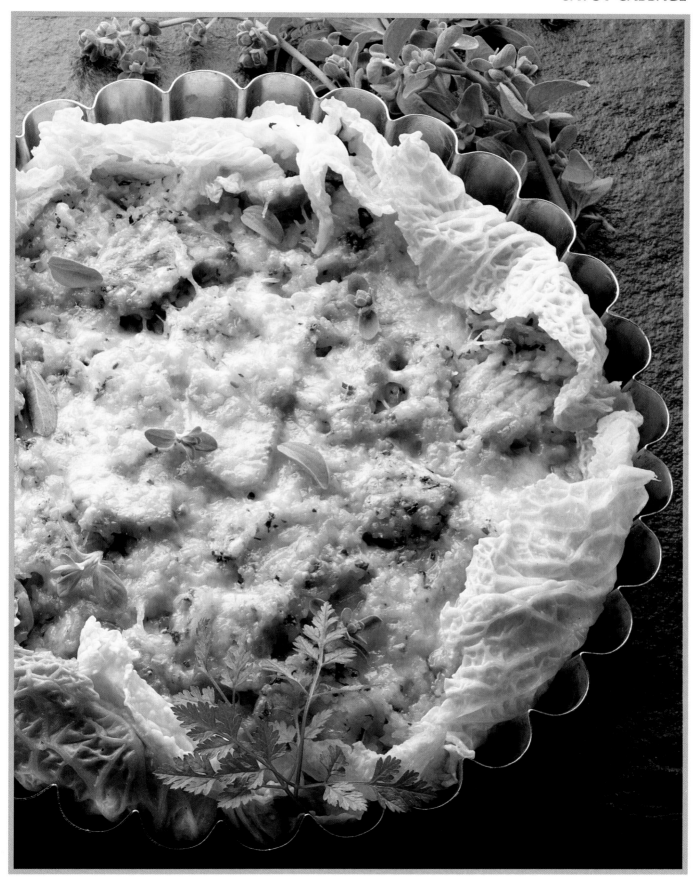

CORNMEAL GNOCCHI WITH HERBS AND FRESH TOMATO SAUCE

SERVES 4 ■■

*Preparation and cooking
time: 1 hour 25 minutes
Kcal per portion: 770
P = 22g, F = 48g, C = 57g*

*750ml/1¼ pints milk
¼ tsp salt
250g/8oz coarse cornmeal
2 eggs
50g/2oz Parmesan or
   Sbrinz cheese
grated nutmeg
50g/2oz butter
4 tbsps chopped fresh herbs
   (rosemary, basil, parsley)
2 garlic cloves
freshly ground white pepper*

FOR THE SAUCE:
*1kg/2¼ lbs very ripe tomatoes
6 basil leaves
6 tbsps cold-pressed olive oil
salt
freshly ground black pepper
1 garlic clove*

1. Bring the milk to the boil with the salt. Add the cornmeal and boil for 40 minutes, stirring frequently. Allow the mixture to cool for 10 minutes, then beat the eggs and stir them into the cornmeal. Fold in the cheese and a little nutmeg. Rinse a baking sheet with cold water. Pour the polenta over it, smooth it out until it is 1cm/⅓ inch thick; leave to cool.
2. Preheat the oven to 220°C/425°F/Gas Mark 7.
3. Using a glass or a biscuit-cutter, cut out half-moon shapes or circles from the polenta. Butter an ovenproof dish and arrange the gnocchi in the dish. Sprinkle with 2 tbsps mixed herbs and the juice of one crushed garlic clove. Sprinkle with a little salt and pepper. Arrange another layer of gnocchi on top, sprinkling with the

Cut half-moon shapes from the polenta dough using a biscuit-cutter or a glass.

Pour melted butter over the polenta.

remaining herbs and the juice of the second garlic clove. Melt the remaining butter, then pour it over the gnocchi.
4. Bake the gnocchi on the centre shelf of the oven or grill them for 15-20 minutes, making sure that the herbs do not burn.
5. Meanwhile, quarter and seed the tomatoes. Purée them in a blender with the basil leaves, then rub the mixture through a sieve to remove the tomato skins. Combine the purée thoroughly with the olive oil, seasoning with salt, pepper and crushed garlic.
Recommended wine: a light, red table wine.

CELERIAC AND ORANGE QUICHE

**MAKES 8 MINIATURE
QUICHES** ■■
*Preparation and cooking
time: 1 hour 40 minutes
Kcal per portion: 480
P = 7g, F = 36g, C = 29g*

FOR THE DOUGH:
*240g/8½oz strong plain flour
½ tsp salt
240g/8½oz butter
120g/4½oz low fat quark*

FOR THE FILLING:
*1 large celeriac root (about
   750g/1lb 10oz)
2 tbsps lemon juice
salt
20g/¾ oz butter
125ml/5 fl oz cream
6 tbsps orange juice
1 tbsp grated untreated
   orange rind
freshly ground white pepper*

*butter for the tartlet tins
1 orange for garnishing*

1. To make the dough, mix the salt and flour together. Cut the butter into pieces, and rub it into the flour using the fingers. Then add the quark and mix well to make a smooth dough, preferably cutting through the mixture with a large knife and then pressing it together. The dough should not be kneaded, as this will make it hard.
2. To make the filling, peel the celeriac, cut it into small pieces and cook with the lemon juice in lightly salted water until soft (about 20 minutes). Drain the celeriac, then purée in a mixer.
3. Preheat the oven to 200°C/400°F/Gas Mark 6.
4. Place the purée with the butter in a pan and cook for 5 minutes, stirring constantly, until the mixture is dry.
5. Add the cream, orange juice and orange rind to the purée. Thicken for a few more minutes, seasoning with salt and pepper.
6. Butter 8 tartlet tins

12cm/4½ inches in diameter. Roll out the dough to a thickness of 3mm/⅛ inch thick and use to line the tartlet tins. Cut out baking foil to fit the tartlet tins and lay it on top of the dough. Then fill them with dried beans or peas and prebake the quiche cases on the centre shelf of the oven for 15 minutes.
7. Fill the quiches with the purée and place them in the oven for a further 10-15 minutes to finish baking.
8. Meanwhile, peel the oranges and remove the white pith. Slice into segments and use to garnish the quiches.
Accompaniment: lamb's lettuce.
Recommended drink: light red table wine or cider.

> **TIP**
>
> *This can also be made into one large quiche, in which case it is important to ensure when baking blind that the pastry is cooked right through. Peas or beans that have been used for baking blind can also be placed in a tin or screw-topped jar once cooled, and used on subsequent occasions. The quiche can be made even more aromatic by adding 1 tbsp bitter orange marmalade to the filling. Spicy seasoning is then required to prevent it from becoming too sweet.*

Wholefood Recipes

*G*rains are a vital element in wholefood cookery. The flour used for pasta, ravioli, pies and pizza should be stone-ground or home-ground, and the dough is home-made. Vegetables and herbs for spicy sauces, delicate fillings and succulent toppings are fresh from the garden or market. Using imagination and culinary skill, this section contains recipes that put an end to the myth of the meagre nut cutlet. Anyone who tries ravioli with cashew nut sauce will never again be drawn by the dubious attractions of processed food, and anyone who experiences the taste of home-made wholewheat pasta with mouth-watering Gorgonzola sauce will undoubtedly be inspired to invest the time and effort needed to try some of the other recipes contained in this chapter.

Rice with Seafood
(see recipe on page 84)

WHOLEWHEAT PASTA WITH GORGONZOLA SAUCE

SERVES 4 ■ ■

Preparation and cooking time: 20 minutes
Standing time: 2 hours
Kcal per portion: 810
P = 22g, F = 50g, C = 58g

FOR THE PASTA DOUGH:
300g/10oz strong wholewheat flour
salt
2-3 eggs
1 tbsp oil
Flour for the work surface

FOR THE SAUCE:
2 small shallots
300ml/12 fl oz veal stock (home made)
300ml /10 fl oz cream
20ml/1½ tbsps sherry vinegar
40ml/3 tbsps sherry
150g/5½oz Gorgonzola
2 tbsps whipped cream

PLUS:
salt
1 tbsp oil

Roll out the wholewheat dough and cut it to the desired shape.

The Gorgonzola is blended into the sauce using a hand-held mixer.

1. To make the dough, sieve the flour and salt into a bowl, make a well in the middle and add 2 eggs and the oil. Stir with a fork, until a dough is formed and then knead by hand or in a food processor. If the dough seems too stiff, add the third egg. Knead until the dough is smooth and shiny. Cover, leave to stand for at least 2 hours and then cut as required.
2. To make the sauce, peel the shallots and cut them into thin rings. Place them in a sauté pan with the veal stock, the cream, sherry vinegar and sherry, and boil over a high heat until the liquid is reduced by a third.
3. Cut the Gorgonzola into small pieces and purée it with the reduced sauce. Then rub the sauce through a fine sieve and bring back to the boil briefly. Finally fold in the whipped cream.
4. Bring a generous amount of water containing salt and oil to the boil in a large pan. Add the pasta and cook it for a few minutes or until al dente.
5. Empty the pasta into a colander, drain well and either mix immediately with the sauce or serve on 4 deep plates and pour the sauce on top.
Recommended wine:
a mature red wine from Piedmont, such as Nebbiolo

TIP

After cooking, pasta must either be drained well and mixed with the sauce, or rinsed briefly under cold running water. It is then heated with a little fat in a large pan before being combined with the sauce.

SPAGHETTI IN RADICCHIO SAUCE

SERVES 4 ■ ■

Preparation and cooking time: 30 minutes
Standing time: 2 hours
Kcal per portion: 820
P = 29g, F = 37g, C = 80g

FOR THE PASTA DOUGH:
500g/1lb 2oz strong wholewheat flour
salt
4-5 eggs
2 tbsps oil
flour for the work surface

FOR THE SAUCE:
200g/7oz radicchio
1 cooking onion
3 tbsps olive oil
40ml/3 tbsps brandy
250ml/8 fl oz beef stock (home made)
125ml/5 fl oz single cream
50g/2oz freshly grated Parmesan
salt
freshly ground white pepper

PLUS:
salt
1 tbsp oil

Remove the stalks before cutting the radicchio leaves into strips.

Sauté the strips of radicchio and onion in olive oil, stirring frequently.

1. Make a pasta dough with the above ingredients, following the method in the previous recipe. Cover, leave to stand for 2 hours and then shape into spaghetti.
2. To make the sauce, remove the outer leaves from the radicchio, which may be withered, cut the head in half and remove the white stalk. Peel the onion, cut it in half, then slice both the radicchio and the onion into fine strips. Set aside 50g/2oz of the radicchio strips.
3. Heat the oil in a sauté pan, add the radicchio and onion strips and sauté over a medium heat, stirring with a wooden spoon. The vegetables must not be allowed to turn brown.
4. As soon as the vegetables are just starting to soften (but still crisp), pour over the brandy, followed by the stock and the cream. Boil, uncovered, over a high heat until the liquid has reduced by a third. Then stir in the Parmesan and season with salt and pepper to taste.
5. Bring a generous amount of water containing salt and oil to the boil in a large pan. Add the spaghetti and cook it for a few minutes until al dente. Drain well in a colander, then transfer it to the pan containing the radicchio sauce, combining the mixture thoroughly using two wooden forks. Serve on 4 plates and garnish with strips of radicchio.
Recommended wine:
a neutral white wine, such as a Riesling.

SWEET RAVIOLI WITH CINNAMON SUGAR

SERVES 4 ■ ■ ■
Preparation and cooking time: 30 minutes
Standing time:2 hours
Kcal per portion: 840
P = 16g, F = 60g, C = 51g

FOR THE PASTA DOUGH:
260g/8½ oz strong
*   wholewheat flour*
pinch of sea salt
2 eggs
1 egg yolk
flour for the work surface

FOR THE FILLING:
250g/8oz plums
1 vanilla pod
50g/2oz chopped almonds
20ml/1½ tbsps plum brandy
1 tsp ground cinnamon
1 tbsp maple syrup

PLUS:
1 egg yolk for coating
salt
1 tbsp oil
200g/7oz butter or margarine
glucose and cinnamon to
*   taste*

Distribute the cooked plum filling evenly over the pasta squares.

Then coat the edges with egg yolk and fold the squares in half.

1. Sift the flour on to a wooden board, sprinkle with salt and make a well in the centre. Add the eggs and the egg yolk, and using a fork, mix the eggs and flour together before kneading into a smooth dough. If the dough is too firm, add another egg; if it is too moist, add a little more flour. Cover and leave to stand for at least 2 hours.
2. To make the filling, cut the plums in half, stone them and dice the flesh finely. Place them in a saucepan. Scrape out the inside of the vanilla pod and stir into the plums. Then add the other ingredients and boil over a low heat until the liquid has evaporated. Remove from the heat and leave to cool.
3. Roll out the pasta dough on a floured board until it is about 1.5mm/¹⁄₁₆ inch thick. Cut it into equal-sized squares, and place a dab of filling on each. Brush the edges of the dough with whisked egg yolk, fold the squares in half and press the edges together firmly.
4. Bring a generous amount of water containing salt and oil to the boil in a large saucepan. Add the ravioli and cook them for a few minutes; as soon as the squares rise to the surface, remove them with a slotted spoon and place them on a heated plate.
5. While the ravioli are cooking, melt the butter or margarine in a pan, then pour it over the ravioli and dust with cinnamon sugar.

RAVIOLI WITH CASHEW NUT SAUCE

SERVES 4 ■ ■ ■
Preparation and cooking time: 45 minutes
Standing time:2 hours
Kcal per portion: 1045
P = 34g, F = 63g, C = 77g

FOR THE PASTA DOUGH:
250g/8oz strong wholewheat
*   flour*
pinch of sea salt
2 eggs
1 egg yolk
flour for the work surface

FOR THE FILLING:
200g/7oz fresh Ricotta
100g/4oz chopped cashew
*   nuts*
salt
freshly ground white pepper

FOR THE SAUCE:
2 garlic cloves
125ml/4 fl oz home-made
*   stock*
125ml/5 fl oz cream
250g/8oz ground cashew nuts

PLUS:
1 egg yolk for coating
salt
1 tbsp oil

1. Make a pasta dough with the above ingredients, following the method given in the previous recipe.
2. For the filling, combine the Ricotta and the nuts thoroughly, seasoning with salt and pepper.
3. Roll out the pasta dough on a floured board until it is about 1.5mm/¹⁄₁₆ inch thick. Cut it into equal-sized squares, and place a dab of filling on each. Brush the edges of the dough with whisked egg yolk, fold the squares in half and press the edges together firmly.
4. To make the sauce, crush or chop the garlic finely, then place it in a high-sided frying pan with the stock and the cream, boiling the mixture over a high heat until

the liquid has reduced by one third. Finally, stir in the ground nuts.
5. Bring a generous amount of water containing salt and oil to the boil in a large saucepan.
6. Cook the ravioli in the boiling salted water for a few minutes. As soon as the squares rise to the surface, remove them with a slotted spoon, serve on 4 preheated plates and pour over the nut sauce.
Recommended wine: a dry Italian white wine, such as Sauvignon from Friuli.

TIP

When preparing the ravioli, the edges must be pressed together very firmly so that none of the filling can escape during cooking. A sufficiently large saucepan should be used so that there is plenty of room for the squares.

WHOLEWHEAT PIZZA WITH
TOMATOES, MOZZARELLA AND BASIL

WHOLEWHEAT PIZZA WITH TOMATOES, MOZZARELLA AND BASIL

SERVES 6 ■ ■

Preparation and cooking time: 1 hour 30 minutes
Rising time: about 2 hours
Kcal per portion: 725
P = 32g, F = 36g, C = 62g

FOR THE DOUGH:
500g/1lb 2oz strong
* wholewheat flour*
30g/1oz fresh yeast
250ml/8 fl oz lukewarm milk
60g/2oz butter, melted
2 eggs, beaten
salt
freshly ground white pepper
flour for the work surface

FOR THE TOPPING:
1 cooking onion
4 tbsps olive oil
450g/1lb canned tomatoes
2 tbsps tomato purée
salt
freshly ground white pepper
1kg/2¼ lbs ripe tomatoes
450g/1lb Mozzarella (made
* from buffalo milk)*
handful of fresh basil
fat for the baking sheet

1. Sift the flour into a bowl, make a well in the centre and crumble in the yeast. Pour in the milk and stir with some of the flour to make a starter. Cover and leave to rise in a warm place for about 30 minutes. Melt the butter and add it to the starter together with the beaten eggs, the salt and pepper. Combine the ingredients and knead until the mixture no longer sticks to the base of the bowl. Cover and leave to rise in a warm place for about 1 hour. The volume of the dough should have doubled by this time.
2. Meanwhile, to make the topping, peel and dice the onion. Heat the oil in a saucepan, add the diced

Stir the wholewheat flour with the yeast and lukewarm milk to make a starter dough.

The best way to combine the ingredients is to use a hand-held mixer with a dough hook.

The volume of the dough will double after rising for 1 hour at room temperature.

Simmer the canned, peeled tomatoes with the sautéed onion for about 10 minutes to combine the mixture thoroughly.

Rub the cooked and seasoned tomato sauce through a fine sieve.

Knead the yeast dough thoroughly once more, then roll it out on a floured, greased baking sheet.

The pizza is first topped with the puréed tomato mixture, then with the pieces of tomato and slices of Mozzarella.

onion and sauté over a medium heat for a few minutes. Chop the canned tomatoes, then add them with their juice and the tomato purée to the pan, season with salt and pepper and simmer the sauce over a low heat for about 10 minutes. Rub the sauce through a broad-meshed sieve and simmer again until a paste forms.
3. Knead the pizza dough thoroughly one more time and again leave to rise for 20 minutes.
4. Blanch the tomatoes briefly, skin them and cut them into eighths, discarding the seeds and the stalk bases. Slice the Mozzarella thinly. Chop the fresh basil finely.
5. Preheat the oven to 220°C/425°F/Gas Mark 7.
6. Roll the dough out on a floured board, then place it on a greased baking sheet. Spread with the tomato sauce, arrange the tomatoes and Mozzarella evenly on top, and finally sprinkle with basil.
7. Bake the pizza on the centre shelf of the oven for 30-40 minutes.
Recommended wine:
a dry white wine, such as a Sauvignon from Friuli.

> ### TIP
>
> *This pizza tastes best with fresh Mozzarella made from buffalo milk, which is sold in small balls. Mozzarella made from cow's milk is not nearly as good.*

MULTI-COLOURED VEGETABLE PIE

SERVES 6-8   ■ ■ ■
Preparation and cooking time: 1 hour 10 minutes
Standing time: 1 hour
Kcal per portion, to serve 6: 800
P = 14g, F = 67g, C = 29g

FOR THE DOUGH:
200g/7oz strong wholewheat flour
1 egg
150g/5¹/₂oz well chilled butter
salt
freshly ground white pepper
flour for the work surface
fat for the oven dish

FOR THE FILLING:
1 red pepper
1 green pepper
1 yellow pepper
3 small courgettes
100g/4oz fresh peas (in the pod)
150g/5¹/₂oz streaky bacon
2 chopped shallots
2 tbsps oil
250g/8oz cherry tomatoes
250ml/8 fl oz single cream
4 eggs
2 tbsps chopped fresh parsley
salt
freshly ground white pepper

1. To make the dough, sift the flour into a bowl, make a well in the centre and add the egg. Place the butter on top of the flour in dabs and sprinkle over some salt and pepper. Knead the mixture to make a smooth dough, then wrap in kitchen foil and place in the refrigerator for 1 hour.
2. For the filling, wash the peppers, cut them in half and remove the stalks and seeds, then dice finely. Wash the courgettes, cut off the ends and slice them finely. Shell the peas and blanch briefly in boiling water.
3. Dice the bacon finely, blanch it briefly, drain well, then add it to the heated oil

Knead the wholewheat flour with the egg and ice-cold pieces of butter to make a dough.

Refrigerate the firm ball of dough for about 1 hour.

Roll the dough out into a round and place in the quiche dish.

Arrange the vegetables in the quiche base.

together with the chopped shallots. Sauté the bacon and shallots over a medium heat for a few minutes, then transfer to a sieve and drain.
4. Preheat the oven to 200°C/400°F/Gas Mark 6.
5. Roll out the dough on a floured board to make a 30cm/12inch round. Line the base and edges of a greased flan case 26cm/10¹/₂ inches in diameter with the dough. Prick several holes in the base using a fork.

> **TIP**
>
> *The pie tastes best when lukewarm, and is ideal for entertaining, as the dough and filling are easy to prepare in advance.*

Arrange two rows of courgette slices upright around the edge. Combine the peppers and peas with the diced bacon and fill the centre of the flan case with the mixture. Wash the cherry tomatoes and dot them over the filling.
6. Whisk the cream and eggs together thoroughly and season with parsley, salt and pepper. Spread the cream mixture over the vegetables and bake the pie on the centre shelf of the oven for about 35 minutes.
Recommended wine:
a German rosé or hock.

QUARK AND NUT FLAN

SERVES 6-8   ■ ■
Preparation and cooking time: 1 hour
Kcal per portion, to serve 6: 825
P = 29g, F = 63g, C = 30g

FOR THE DOUGH:
200g/7oz strong wholewheat flour
1 egg
150g/5¹/₂oz well chilled butter
salt
freshly ground white pepper
flour for the work surface
fat for the oven dish

FOR THE FILLING:
100g/4oz pistachio nuts
100g/4oz pine kernels
500g/1lb 2oz Mascarpone
300g/10oz low-fat quark
125g/5oz crème fraîche
4 eggs
salt
freshly ground white pepper
freshly grated nutmeg

1. Sift the flour into a bowl, make a well in the centre and add the egg. Place the butter on top of the flour in dabs and sprinkle over some salt and pepper. Knead the mixture briskly to make a smooth dough, then wrap in kitchen foil and place in the refrigerator for 1 hour.
2. For the topping, roast the nuts in a pan, then chop them finely.
3. Combine the Mascarpone, quark, crème fraîche and eggs. Season with salt, pepper and nutmeg, then stir in the nuts.
4. Preheat the oven to 200°C/400°F/Gas Mark 6.
5. Roll out the dough on a floured board to make a circle 30cm/12 inches in diameter. Line the base and edges of a greased flan case 26cm/10¹/₂ inches in diameter with the dough. Prick several holes in the base using a fork. Spread the filling over the dough and bake the flan on the centre shelf of the oven for 35-40 minutes.
Recommended wine:
a dry Silvaner.

VARIATIONS ON RISOTTO

Basic Recipe

SERVES 4 ■
Preparation and cooking time: 35 minutes
Kcal per portion: 290
P = 6g, F = 12g, C = 37g

1 onion
3 tbsps grapeseed oil
200g/7oz short-grain brown rice
750ml/1¼ pints home-made stock

Peel and dice the onion. Heat the oil in a pan, add the onion and sauté over a medium heat for a few minutes. Then add the rice and slowly pour over the stock. Cook the rice over a low heat for 15-20 minutes.

Risotto with Peas and Spinach

Kcal per portion: 695
P = 23g, F = 42g, C = 50g

1 portion of cooked rice

250ml/8 fl oz single cream
300g/10oz cooked spinach
400g/14oz cooked peas
salt
freshly ground white pepper
fat for the oven dish
100g/4oz freshly grated Parmesan

Boil the cream over a high heat to reduce the liquid, then stir in the spinach and 200g/7oz peas. Season with salt and pepper. Purée the mixture in a blender, then rub it through a sieve. Preheat the grill. Stir the vegetable and cream purée together with the remaining peas into the rice, seasoning with salt and pepper. Transfer the mixture to a greased oven dish. Sprinkle with cheese and grill for 3-4 minutes.

Peas and spinach add a tasty touch to risotto.

Spring onions and sprouted seeds are perfect ingredients for risotto.

Shiitake mushrooms may be used in risotto.

Dates and raisins make a sweet variation.

Peppers also add flair to risotto.

Herbs and pumpkin seeds go well with rice.

Sultanas and nuts go well with risotto.

Risotto with Shiitake Mushrooms

Kcal per portion: 375
P = 7g, F = 20g, C = 40g

1 portion of cooked rice

200g/7oz fresh shiitake mushrooms
3 tbsps grapeseed oil
2 chopped shallots
salt
freshly ground white pepper
a bunch of chives, chopped finely

Clean the mushrooms and dice them finely. Heat the grapeseed oil in a saucepan, add the diced shallots and sauté for a few minutes. Then add the mushrooms, sauté for a further 3-4 minutes, and season with salt and pepper. Stir in the cooked rice and chives, heating the mixture through briefly.

Risotto with Mixed Peppers

Kcal per portion: 430
P = 9g, F = 23g, C = 44g

1 portion of cooked rice

2 red peppers
2 green peppers
2 yellow peppers
2 shallots
4 tbsps olive oil
salt
freshly ground white pepper

Wash the peppers, cut them in half, remove the stalks and seeds and dice finely. Peel the shallots and chop them finely. Heat the olive oil in a saucepan, add the diced vegetables, and sauté for a few minutes over a high heat. Season with salt and pepper, then continue cooking over a medium heat for 5-6 minutes, stirring frequently. Finally stir in the rice and heat the mixture through briefly.

Risotto with Nuts and Currants

Kcal per portion: 475
P = 8g, F = 27g, C = 46g

1 portion of cooked rice

3 tbsps hazelnut oil
50g/2oz chopped hazelnuts
50g/2oz currants
salt
freshly ground white pepper

Use hazelnut oil instead of the grapeseed oil given in the basic risotto recipe.
Mix the cooked rice with the nuts and raisins, season with salt and pepper and heat through.
An accompaniment for exotic dishes.

Risotto with Spring Onions and Sprouts

Kcal per portion: 545
P = 23g, F = 42g, C = 38g

1 portion of cooked rice

a bunch of spring onions
3 tbsps grapeseed oil
200g/7oz mixed grain sprouts
salt
freshly ground white pepper
fat for the oven dish
200g/7oz freshly grated Emmental

Preheat the grill. Clean and wash the spring onions, then slice them finely, including some of the green leaves. Heat the grapeseed oil in a saucepan, add the spring onions and sauté for 1-2 minutes. Then add the rice and season with salt and pepper. Finally stir in the sprouts.
Transfer the rice mixture to a greased oven dish, sprinkle with cheese and grill for 3-4 minutes.

Risotto with Dates and Raisins

Kcal per portion: 510
P = 9g, F = 26g, C = 56g

1 portion of cooked rice

100g/4oz small pearl onions
salt
2 tbsps olive oil
freshly ground white pepper
50g/2oz dates
50g/2oz raisins
50g/2oz chopped almonds

Peel the onions and cook them in a little salted water for about 3-5 minutes until they are just starting to soften (but still crisp).
Heat the olive oil in a saucepan, add the onions and sauté over a medium heat for a few minutes. Then add the cooked rice and season with salt and pepper. Peel, stone and chop the dates. Stir them with the raisins and almonds into the rice, mix well and heat through.
An accompaniment to rice dishes.

Risotto with Desiccated Coconut

Kcal per portion: 525
P = 8g, F = 35g, C = 40g

1 portion of cooked rice
3 tbsps olive oil
100g/4oz desiccated coconut
1 tbsp chopped fresh lemon balm
1 tsp chopped untreated lemon rind
1 tsp turmeric
salt
freshly ground white pepper

Prepare the rice as indicated in the basic recipe, but use olive oil for frying instead of grapeseed oil. Stir in the desiccated coconut, herbs and spices, then heat the mixture through briefly.
An accompaniment to poultry dishes.

Risotto with Pumpkin Seeds and Herbs

Kcal per portion: 570
P = 11g, F = 38g, C = 40g

1 portion of cooked rice

250ml/8 fl oz cream
100g/4oz roasted pumpkin seeds
2 tbsps chopped fresh chervil
bunch of finely chopped chives
1 tbsp finely chopped fresh borage
salt
freshly ground black pepper

Prepare the rice as indicated in the basic recipe, but replace 250ml/8 fl oz of the stock with the cream. Stir the pumpkin seeds and the herbs into the cooked rice and season with salt and pepper.
An accompaniment to egg dishes.

TIP

Pumpkin seeds taste nutty and flavoursome. They contain valuable fat, highly nutritious protein, and are rich in vitamins and minerals. In natural medicine, they have been used for centuries to treat urinary tract disorders. The oily seeds have a limited storage life, and are best kept in a cool, dark place.

WHEAT RISOTTO WITH KOHLRABI

SERVES 4 ■■
Preparation and cooking time: 40 minutes
Kcal per portion: 295
P = 9g, F = 16g, C = 27g

6 tbsps olive oil
150g/5½ oz wheat grains
2 chopped shallots
1 chopped garlic clove
750ml/1¼ pints home-made stock (beef, poultry or vegetable)
2 small kohlrabi
1 red pepper
half a bunch of celery
1 courgette
salt
freshly ground white pepper
handful of fresh chervil
handful of fresh parsley

1. Heat 2 tbsps olive oil in a saucepan, add the wheat grains, the shallots and garlic, and sauté for a few minutes over a medium heat. Pour over the stock, and cook the wheat for 45 minutes over a low heat.
2. Meanwhile, peel the kohlrabi, halve the pepper, and remove the stem and seeds. Divide the celery into individual sticks, and wash both the celery and the courgettes. Then dice all the vegetables finely, add them to a pan containing the remaining oil, and cook over a medium heat for about 5 minutes. Season with salt and pepper.
3. Chop the herbs finely, then stir them together with the diced vegetables into the cooked wheat grains. Season before serving.

RICE WITH SEAFOOD

Photo, page 72

SERVES 4   ■ ■
Preparation time:
30 minutes
Marinating time:
30 minutes
Kcal per portion: 810
P = 22g, F = 33g, C = 99g

1/2 cucumber
100g/4oz celery
100g/4oz fresh mushrooms
200g/7oz cooked short-grain
brown rice
salt
freshly ground white pepper
1 tsp ground turmeric
20ml/1 1/2 tbsps soy sauce
40ml/2 1/2 tbsps rice wine or
sherry fino
50ml/3 1/2 tbsps sherry vinegar
50ml/3 1/2 tbsps rice vinegar
50ml/3 1/2 tbsps sesame oil
150ml/4 1/2 fl oz grapeseed oil

PLUS:
4 small crayfish
4 small squid (calamari)
2 tbsps olive oil
8 fresh oysters, shelled

1. Wash the cucumber and celery, clean the mushrooms and dice all three finely. Combine with the rice in a bowl.
2. To make the dressing, mix the salt, pepper and turmeric with the soy sauce, rice wine and vinegar until the salt dissolves. Then stir in the oils. Pour the dressing over the salad ingredients, mix well and leave to marinate for half an hour.
3. Shell the crayfish, wash the squid and pat them dry. Heat the olive oil, add the seafood and fry for 2 minutes, turning once. Poach the oysters for half a minute in hot salted water, then stir them along with the other seafood into the rice salad.
Recommended wine:
Sancerre or Chardonnay.

RICE RISSOLES

SERVES 4   ■
Preparation time:
1 hour
Kcal per portion: 500
P = 13g, F = 28g, C = 46g

200g/7oz short-grain brown
rice
salt
2 chopped shallots
50g/2oz freshly-grated
Parmesan
2 eggs
50g/2oz breadcrumbs
a bunch of chives, finely
chopped
freshly ground white pepper
100g/4oz clarified butter or
margarine

1. Bring the rice to the boil in 500ml/16 fl oz water placed in a sealed pressure cooker. Cook over a low heat for about 15 minutes.
2. Place the cooked rice in a bowl and leave to cool. Then mix with diced shallots and Parmesan, gradually stir in the eggs, and add enough breadcrumbs to make a mass that can be shaped. Season with chives, salt and pepper.
3. Shape the mixture into rissoles with a diameter of about 5cm/2 inches. Heat the fat in a non-stick pan, add the rissoles and fry over a medium heat on both sides for 1-2 minutes until golden brown.
An accompaniment to fish and poultry dishes or vegetable ragoûts or, served with a light sauce, as a main meal.

SPELT DUMPLINGS

SERVES 6   ■
Preparation time:
30 minutes
Standing time:
30 minutes
Kcal per portion: 270
P = 10g, F = 11g, C = 29g

750ml/1 1/4 pints home-made
stock
50g/2oz butter
100g/4oz spelt flour
100g/4oz strong wholewheat
flour
50g/2oz spelt grains or bulgar
wheat, soaked for 2 hours
1 tsp crushed coriander seeds
4 eggs
salt
freshly ground white pepper

1. Bring the stock and butter to the boil in a saucepan. Stir in the flours and grains and the crushed coriander seeds; continue stirring over a medium heat until a smooth lump is formed which no longer sticks to the base of the pan.
2. Remove the pan from the heat and gradually stir in the eggs until the dough is completely smooth. Season with salt and pepper and leave to stand for 30 minutes.
3. Bring a generous amount of salted water to the boil in a large saucepan. Shape the spelt dough into small dumplings and cook them in the boiling salted water for 10 minutes over a low heat. Serve as an accompaniment to mushroom dishes with sauce or spring vegetables in chervil sauce.

OAT SLICES

SERVES 4   ■ ■
Preparation time:
1 hour 15 minutes
Kcal per portion: 585
P = 17g, F = 32g, C = 52g

1 shallot
1 medium-sized carrot
100g/4oz celeriac
100g/4oz clarified butter or
margarine
250g/8oz porridge oats
750ml/1 1/4 pints stock
salt
1 tsp finely chopped thyme
leaves
freshly ground white pepper
freshly grated nutmeg
2 eggs
fat for the oven dish
50g/2oz rolled oats

1. Peel the shallots. Clean, wash and dice the carrot and celery. Heat 50g/2oz fat, add the diced vegetables and sauté for a few minutes. Scatter the porridge oats into the pan, sauté briefly, then pour over the stock. Season with salt and cook for about 10 minutes over a low heat. Transfer to a bowl and leave to cool.
2. Preheat the oven to 200°C/400°F/Gas Mark 6.
3. Stir the spices and eggs into the oats and vegetables. Then place the mixture in a greased springform 24cm/9 1/2 inches in diameter and bake on the centre shelf of the oven for 30 minutes.
4. Heat the remaining clarified butter or margarine in a pan, add the rolled oats, sauté for a few minutes and then spread evenly over the oat and vegetable mixture. Bake for a further 10 minutes until crispy. Leave to cool a little, then cut into slices. An accompaniment to meat or vegetable dishes.

Quick-and-easy Recipes

*T*he recipes in this chapter would not discredit the menu of the most sophisticated restaurant, and even lend themselves to festive occasions. What all of them have in common is that they are quick to prepare. It is not necessary to spend hours slaving over a hot stove to produce a sophisticated and innovative meal.

Pasta dishes such as Rigatoni with Parsley and Nut Sauce, Tortellini with Tomato and Basil Sauce and many other pasta variations can be cooked and served appetizingly in an instant. Even unexpected guests can be catered for without elaborate preparations, using all types of cereal-based dishes such as Herb Pizza with Mozzarella, Quiche with Chives, or Cress Pies. No-one will be able to guess from the finished dish that it was featured as a quick recipe idea.

Barley and Vegetables with Smoked Pork Loin (see recipe on page 96)

ELBOW MACARONI WITH COURGETTES

SERVES 4 ■
Preparation time: 30 minutes
Kcal per portion: 775
P = 21g, F = 43g, C = 69g

400g/14oz elbow macaroni
salt
30g/1oz butter
1 large onion, chopped
150g/5½oz streaky bacon
200g/7oz courgettes
4 eggs
freshly ground black pepper
a bunch of chives, chopped
*   finely*

1. Cook the pasta in a generous quantity of salted water for 5-7 minutes until al dente, then drain in a sieve.
2. Meanwhile, heat the butter in a large sauté pan, add the chopped onion and sauté until transparent. Cut the bacon into narrow strips, removing the rind, and fry with the onions.
3. Wash the courgettes, cut off the ends and grate coarsely directly over the pan. Sauté for 8 minutes, stirring frequently. Season with salt and pepper.
4. Break the eggs into a bowl and beat using an egg whisk.
5. Stir the pasta into the courgette mixture. Pour over the eggs and cook over a medium heat for 8-10 minutes, stirring frequently, and scattering in the chives.
Accompaniment: lamb's lettuce with radishes.
Recommended drink: Beer or dry cider.

PENNE WITH PEA AND CREAM SAUCE

SERVES 4 ■
Preparation and cooking time: 25 minutes
Kcal per portion: 905
P = 35g, F = 40g, C = 94g

30g/1oz butter
1 onion, chopped
300g/10oz frozen peas
300ml/10 fl oz cream
250g/8oz cooked ham
salt
freshly ground black pepper
a pinch of freshly-grated
*   nutmeg*
1-2 tsps lemon juice
500g/1lb 2oz penne
handful of fresh mint

1. Cook the penne in a generous quantity of salted water for 10-12 minutes until al dente.
2. Meanwhile, heat the butter in a medium-sized pan, add the diced onion and sauté until transparent. Then add the peas and cream and simmer for 8-10 minutes.
3. Cut the ham into narrow strips and stir it into the sauce just before the end of the cooking time. Season generously with salt, pepper, nutmeg and lemon juice. Wash the mint, pluck the leaves from the stems and sprinkle them in the sauce.
4. Drain the pasta and combine with the sauce in a large bowl.
Accompaniment: freshly grated Parmesan, fennel salad with black olives.
Recommended wine: a light, red table wine.

SPAGHETTI WITH SPINACH SAUCE

SERVES 4 ■
Preparation and cooking time: 25 minutes
Kcal per portion: 680
P = 29g, F = 20g, C = 94g

2 tbsps olive oil
1 onion, chopped
300g/10oz frozen, chopped
spinach
250ml/8 fl oz meat stock
*   (instant)*
500g/1lb 2oz spaghetti
salt
freshly ground black pepper
freshly grated nutmeg
1 tsp oregano, fresh or dried
200g/7oz Feta cheese
2 tbsps pine kernels

1. Heat the olive oil in a medium-sized pan, add the diced onion and fry until transparent. Then add the spinach, pour over the meat stock and simmer for 15 minutes, stirring occasionally.
2. Cook the spaghetti in a generous quantity of salted water for 8-10 minutes until al dente, then drain.
3. Season the spinach with salt, pepper, nutmeg and oregano.
4. Crumble the Feta cheese or chop it roughly. Then stir it into the spinach and simmer for a further 5 minutes. Scatter in the pine kernels and season once more.
5. Serve the spaghetti on 4 plates, topping it with the sauce.
Accompaniment: tomato salad with vinaigrette.
Recommended wine: a light, red table wine.

RIGATONI WITH PARSLEY AND NUT SAUCE

SERVES 4 ■
Preparation time:
20 minutes
Kcal per portion: 860
P = 27g, F = 42g, C = 88g

30g/1oz butter
1 onion, chopped
100g/4oz walnuts, chopped
500g/1lb 2oz rigatoni
salt
200g/7oz full-fat cream
*   cheese*
200ml/6 fl oz cream
freshly ground black pepper
1 tsp thyme, fresh or dried
1-2 tsps lemon juice
large handful of curly-
*   leaved parsley, finely*
*   chopped*

1. Heat the butter in a medium-sized pan, add the chopped onion, and sauté until transparent. Then add the chopped walnuts.
2. Cook the rigatoni in boiling salted water for 10-12 minutes until al dente. Drain and transfer to a large bowl.
3. Meanwhile, stir the cheese and the cream into the onion and nut mixture, bring to the boil and simmer over a low heat until the pasta is ready. Season with salt, pepper, thyme and lemon juice.
4. Stir the parsley into the sauce, then season once more. Either serve the sauce separately or pour it over the pasta; mix well and serve immediately.
Accompaniment: tomato salad with onions.
Recommended wine: a light, red table wine, such as Chianti or Beaujolais.

TORTELLINI WITH TOMATO AND BASIL SAUCE

SERVES 4 ■
Preparation and cooking time: 25 minutes
Kcal per portion: 540
P = 20g, F = 9g, C = 92g

2 tbsps olive oil
1 onion, chopped
4 sticks of celery
2 carrots
500g/1lb 2oz canned
   tomatoes, sieved
2 garlic cloves
salt
freshly ground black pepper
1 bay leaf
1 tsp each of oregano and
   thyme, fresh or dried
500g/1lb 2oz tortellini
handful of fresh basil

1. Heat the olive oil in a saucepan. Add the diced onion and sauté until transparent.
2. Wash the celery, remove any tough threads, and slice

TIP

If any of the sauce is left over, it can be made into a salad dressing by adding oil and vinegar. 250g/8oz minced pork could be fried with the onions to make the sauce richer and tastier.

thinly. Place it in the saucepan with the onions. Peel the carrots and grate them coarsely into the pan. Sauté the mixture for 5 minutes.
3. Add the tomatoes to the pan. Peel the garlic and crush it directly into the pan. Season the sauce with salt, pepper, the bay leaf, oregano and thyme, then

Grate the carrots using a coarse grater.

Remove the strings on the outside of the celery sticks using a knife.

simmer for 10 minutes.
4. Meanwhile, cook the tortellini for 10-15 minutes in accordance with the instructions on the packet.
5. Season the sauce once more, remove the bay leaf and throw it away. Rinse the basil, pluck the leaves from the stems and scatter into the sauce just before serving. Serve the sauce separately from the tortellini.
Accompaniment: freshly grated Parmesan and green bean salad.
Recommended wine: a light red or rosé wine.

FARFALLE WITH BEAN SAUCE

SERVES 4 ■
Preparation and cooking time: 20 minutes
Kcal per portion: 585
P = 28g, F = 8g, C = 96g

1 tbsp olive oil
1 onion, chopped
3 garlic cloves
1 small can of red kidney
   beans (225g/7½oz when
   drained)
4 tbsps Mascarpone
400g/14oz farfalle
salt
freshly ground black pepper
pinch of cayenne pepper
1 tsp grated rind of an
   untreated lemon
juice of ½ lemon
1 carton cress

1. Heat the olive oil in a saucepan. Add the chopped onion and sauté until transparent. Peel and crush the garlic and add it to the onion.
2. Drain the beans in a sieve. Then purée with Mascarpone in a blender. Add the purée to the saucepan and simmer for 10 minutes.
3. Meanwhile, cook the pasta in a generous quantity of salted water for 10-12 minutes until al dente, then drain.
4. Season the bean sauce generously with salt, pepper, cayenne pepper, lemon rind and lemon juice. Rinse the cress and, using kitchen scissors, cut the leaves over the sauce just before serving. Serve the pasta separately from the sauce.
Accompaniment: Freshly grated Parmesan, mangetout salad with vinaigrette.
Recommended wine: a dry red wine, such as Côtes du Rhône or Corbières.

TAGLIATELLE WITH TOMATO AND ROCKET SAUCE

SERVES 4 ■
Preparation and cooking time: 25 minutes
Kcal per portion: 610
P = 26g, F = 15g, C = 89g

2 tbsps olive oil
1 onion, chopped
1 small can of tomatoes
   (210g/7oz when drained)
500g/1lb 2oz tagliatelle
salt
freshly ground black pepper
100g/4oz rocket plant
1 ball of Mozzarella
   (150g/5½oz)

1. Heat the olive oil in a medium-sized pan, add the chopped onion, and fry until transparent. Then add the tomatoes, together with their juice, chop them roughly in the pan and simmer for 10 minutes.
2. Cook the pasta in a generous quantity of boiling salted water for 8-10 minutes until al dente.
3. Rinse the rocket, leave the small leaves whole and chop

TIP

Rocket is not always easy to find, so coriander may be used as a substitute.

the larger ones. First slice and then dice the Mozzarella.
4. Season the tomato sauce with salt and pepper, then fold in the rocket and diced Mozzarella.
5. Drain the pasta, serve on 4 plates and top with the sauce.
Accompaniment: salad.
Recommended wine: a light red wine, such as Chianti.

BEAN THREADS WITH CHICKEN BREAST AND MINT

SERVES 4 ■
Preparation and cooking time: 25 minutes
Kcal per portion: 560
$P = 38g, \ F = 26g, \ C = 37g$

200g/7oz bean threads
4 chicken breast fillets
45g/1½oz clarified butter
1 small chilli
3 garlic cloves
100g/4oz salted peanuts
juice of 1 lemon
freshly ground white pepper
pinch of ground coriander
handful of fresh mint

Lay the bean threads in a pan and pour boiling water over them.

Fry the chicken with the chilli over a high heat, then add the garlic and peanuts.

Drain the cooked bean threads and chop them with a pair of scissors.

Stir the bean threads into the pan.

1. Blanch the bean threads with boiling water and leave to soak for 10 minutes. (If the instructions on the packet are different, then these should be observed.)
2. If necessary, remove the skin and fat from the chicken breast fillets. Cut them cross-ways into slices ½cm/¼ inch thick.
3. Heat the clarified butter in a high-sided frying pan. Crush the chilli with the back of a knife and place it in the pan. Then add the chicken and fry over a high heat for 3 minutes. Peel and crush the garlic, adding it to the pan. Scatter in the peanuts.
4. Pour the bean threads into a sieve and drain. Chop them into shorter lengths using a pair of kitchen scissors and stir them into the pan. Season generously with lemon juice, pepper and coriander, then fry for 5 minutes.
5. Wash the mint, pluck off the leaves and use to garnish.
Accompaniment: soya bean sprout and cress salad.
Recommended wine: a dry white wine.

TUNA AND COURGETTE PIZZA

SERVES 4 ■
Preparation and cooking time: 40 minutes
Kcal per portion: 660
$P = 35g, \ F = 37g, \ C = 39g$

fat for the baking sheet
300g/10oz yeast dough (chilled fresh dough)
500g/1lb 2oz beef tomatoes
salt
freshly ground black pepper
2 courgettes (350g/11oz)
2 cans of tuna in natural juice (2 x 185g/6½oz)
1 ball of Mozzarella (150g/5½oz)
oregano for scattering over the top
olive oil for sprinkling over the top

1. Grease a baking sheet. Roll the dough out thinly on the tray, making a thicker rim around the edge.
2. Preheat the oven to 200°C/400°F/Gas Mark 6.
3. Blanch, skin and seed the tomatoes, then chop them roughly. Spread them over the yeast dough and season with salt and pepper.
4. Wash the courgettes, cut off the ends and slice very finely. Spread evenly over the tomatoes.
5. Drain the tuna and break it up with a fork. Arrange it over the courgettes.
6. Dice the Mozzarella finely and scatter it on top. Season with oregano and sprinkle with olive oil. Bake on the bottom shelf of the oven for 25 minutes.
Recommended drink: beer or a light, red table wine.

FRIED BEAN THREADS WITH SHRIMPS

SERVES 4 ■
Preparation time: 25 minutes
Kcal per portion: 310
$P = 18g, F = 10g, C = 35g$

200g/7oz bean threads
1 small Chinese cabbage (250g/8oz)
3 tbsps soya oil
2 garlic cloves
4 tbsps soy sauce
freshly ground black pepper
1 tsp Chinese five-spice
200g/7oz shrimps (from a jar or can)
handful of lemon balm

1. Blanch the bean threads with boiling water and leave them to soak for 10 minutes. Pour them into a sieve, drain thoroughly and cut them with kitchen scissors.
2. Clean and quarter the Chinese cabbage, cut it into very fine strips, wash and drain well.
3. Heat the soya oil in a wok or frying pan. Add the Chinese cabbage and fry for 8 minutes. Stir in the bean threads. Peel the garlic, crush it directly into the pan, and fry for a further 5 minutes. Season generously with the soy sauce, pepper and Chinese five-spice; the bean threads absorb a lot of flavour.
4. Stir in the shrimps and heat through for 3 minutes.
5. Rinse the lemon balm, pluck the leaves from the stems and stir them gently into the bean thread mixture.
Accompaniment: mushroom salad with vinaigrette.
Recommended wine: a dry white wine.

PIZZA WITH OLIVES AND SARDINES

SERVES 4 ■
Preparation and cooking time: 35 minutes
Kcal per portion: 420
P = 17g, F = 21g, C = 37g

fat for the baking sheet
300g/10oz yeast dough
  (chilled fresh dough)
250g/8oz sieved tomatoes
  (canned)
salt
freshly ground black pepper
2 garlic cloves
150g/5¹/₂oz stoned, green
  olives
2 cans filleted sardines
2 tsps oregano
4 tbsps Emmental, freshly
  grated

1. Grease a baking sheet. Roll out the dough on the tray, making a raised rim around the edge.
2. Boil the tomatoes for 8 minutes. Season with salt and pepper. Peel the garlic and crush it into the pan.

TIP

For parties, you can make about 20 mini-pizzas from the same quantity of dough.

3. Preheat the oven to 200°C/400°F/Gas Mark 6.
4. Slice the olives and drain the sardines in a sieve.
5. Cover the dough evenly with the tomatoes. Divide the sardines into pieces and lay them on the tomatoes. Scatter over the olives. Season with salt, pepper and oregano. Sprinkle the Emmental on top. Bake on the lower shelf of the oven for 20-25 minutes.
Recommended wine:
a red Italian table wine.

Roll the dough out directly on the baking sheet.

Crush the garlic into the cooked tomato purée.

Lay the sardines on the tomato purée, then scatter over the olives.

Before baking, spoon the grated Emmental over the pizza.

MINCED MEAT PIZZA WITH GORGONZOLA

SERVES 4 ■
Preparation and cooking time: 35 minutes
Kcal per portion: 760
P = 34g, F = 47g, C = 42g

2 tbsps olive oil
1 onion, chopped
2 garlic cloves
400g/14oz minced meat
5 tbsps tomato purée
1 tsp each of thyme and
  oregano, fresh or dried
fat for the baking sheet
300g/10oz yeast dough
  (chilled fresh dough)
200g/7oz full-fat Gorgonzola

1. Heat the olive oil in a pan, add the chopped onion and fry until transparent. Peel the garlic clove and crush it into the pan. Add the meat and fry until it is crumbly. Stir in the tomato purée and season with salt, pepper and herbs.
2. Preheat the oven to 200°C/400°F/Gas Mark 6.
3. Grease a baking sheet and roll the dough out on it, making the edge slightly higher than the base. Spread the meat out over the dough and top with dabs of Gorgonzola.
4. Place the pizza on the bottom shelf of the oven and bake for 20 minutes.
The dough may also be divided into portions before adding the topping, to make small individual pizzas.
Recommended wine:
a light red wine from Italy or France.

HERB PIZZA WITH MOZZARELLA

SERVES 4 ■
Preparation and cooking time: 35 minutes
Kcal per portion: 935
P = 36g, F = 45g, C = 96g

FOR THE DOUGH:
250g/8oz low-fat quark
salt
5 tbsps olive oil
2 eggs
500g/1lb 2oz flour
fat for the baking sheet

FOR THE TOPPING:
large handful each of
  chives, parsley and basil
200g/7oz crème fraîche
1 egg
freshly ground black pepper
2 balls of Mozzarella
  (150g/5¹/₂oz each)

1. To make the dough, mix the quark in a bowl with a generous pinch of salt, the olive oil and eggs, to make a smooth mass. Add the flour and work it into the mixture until all the ingredients have combined to make a malleable dough.
2. Preheat the oven to 220°C/425°F/Gas Mark 7.
3. Grease a baking sheet and roll out the dough on the tray, raising the edges and pricking the base several times with a fork.
4. Chop the herbs finely and combine them with the crème fraîche and the egg. Season with salt and pepper and spread over the dough. Chop the Mozzarella into 1-cm/³/₈ inch thick slices, then dice and scatter over the top.
5. Bake the pizza on the bottom shelf of the oven for 15 minutes. Serve immediately.
Recommended wine:
a light red wine, such as Chianti.

CRESS PIES

SERVES 4 ■

*Preparation and cooking
time: 35 minutes
Kcal per portion: 335
P = 11g, F = 21g, C = 23g*

*200g/7oz packaged dough to
    make 4 rolls (chilled fresh
    dough)
fat for the baking sheet
200g/7oz full-fat cream
    cheese with herbs
1 small onion
freshly ground black pepper
2 cartons cress*

1. Take the 4 pieces of dough out of their packet and place on a greased baking sheet. Press each of them slightly flat with the ball of the hand to make a well in the centre.
2. Preheat the oven to 200°C/400°F/Gas Mark 6.
3. Dice the cream cheese finely and place it on the pieces of dough. Peel the onions, chop them into rings and arrange them on top. Season with pepper.
4. Bake the pies on the centre shelf of the oven for about 25 minutes.
5. Wash and chop the cress, scatter thickly on top of the pies, and serve.

TIP

*Instead of cress,
it is of course
possible to use
other fresh herbs.
Likewise, the
cream cheese
may be replaced
by sheep's cheese.
These pies are
ideal for a lavish
Sunday brunch.*

CURRIED RICE WITH TURKEY

SERVES 4 ■

*Preparation and cooking
time: 25 minutes
Kcal per portion: 710
P = 37g, F = 25g, C = 79g*

*30g/1oz clarified butter
1 large onion, chopped
400g/14oz turkey breast
    fillets
2 tbsps curry powder
100g/4oz almonds, chopped
3 tbsps raisins
750ml/1¼ pints chicken
    stock (instant)
salt
freshly ground black pepper
300g/10oz easy-cook rice
2 tbsps dessicated coconut
1 banana*

1. Heat the clarified butter in a large saucepan. Add the chopped onion and sauté until transparent.
2. Cut the turkey into narrow strips, add it to the pan and fry over a high heat for a few minutes. Sprinkle over the curry powder and sauté it in the fat.
3. Stir in the almonds and raisins. Pour over the chicken stock, bring to the boil, and season with salt and pepper. Add the easy-cook rice, cover the pan and cook over a medium heat for 5 minutes.
4. Sprinkle in the desiccated coconut. Peel and slice the banana and add to the pan. Season once more, and serve garnished either with chopped fresh coriander or parsley.
Accompaniment: cucumber salad with yoghurt sauce.
Recommended drink: beer or Gewürztraminer, or the Indian yoghurt drink, lassi.

QUICHE WITH CHIVES

SERVES 4 ■

*Preparation and cooking
time: 35 minutes
Kcal per portion: 680
P = 23g, F = 47g, C = 34g*

*250g/8oz short-crust pastry
    dough (chilled fresh dough)
flour for the work surface
fat for the baking sheet
200ml/7 fl oz sour cream
4 eggs
salt
freshly ground black pepper
freshly grated nutmeg
3 bunches chives
2 onions
150g/5½oz grated Gouda*

1. Preheat the oven to 220°C/425°F/Gas Mark 7.
2. Roll the dough out on a floured work surface. Grease a springform 26cm/10½ inches in diameter and line it with the dough, making an edge about 3cm/1¼ inches high, and pricking the base with a fork several times. Prebake on the centre shelf of the oven for 10 minutes.
3. Meanwhile, mix the sour cream with the eggs in a bowl. Season generously with salt, pepper and nutmeg. Wash and dry the chives, chop finely and stir into the cream and egg mixture.
4. Peel the onion, slice it into fine rings and arrange them over the prebaked dough. Then pour over the cream and egg mixture and sprinkle cheese on top. Bake for a further 25 minutes. Serve garnished with chives.
Recommended drink: a chilled Pils.

BARLEY AND VEGETABLES WITH SMOKED PORK LOIN

Photo, page 86/87

SERVES 4 ■■

*Preparation and cooking
time: 30 minutes
Kcal per portion: 370
P = 19g, F = 19g, C = 27g*

*150g/5½oz pot barley
salt
2 carrots
3 tbsps olive oil
2 leeks
300g/10oz smoked pork loin,
    in ½ cm/¼ inch thick slices
freshly ground black pepper
1 tsp thyme, fresh or dried*

1. Bring 750ml/1¼ pints water to the boil in a large saucepan. Add the barley, season with salt, cover and simmer for 20 minutes.
2. Peel the carrots. Heat the olive oil in a large saucepan. Using a cucumber slicer, slice the carrots finely straight into the pan.
3. Clean the leek, cut it in half lengthways, wash thoroughly and slice finely. Then add it to the pan with the carrots and sauté for 10 minutes.
4. Dice the pork finely and stir it into the mixture.
5. Pour the barley into a sieve, drain, then combine with the contents of the pan. Season generously with salt, pepper and thyme.
Accompaniment: lukewarm bean salad with onions.
Recommended drink: beer.

TIP

*Cold barley makes
an ideal salad
combined with
various vegetables
and mushrooms.*

OYSTER MUSHROOM QUICHE

SERVES 4 ■

Preparation and cooking time: 35 minutes
Kcal per portion: 685
P = 15g, F = 49g, C = 43g

2 tbsps olive oil
1 onion, chopped
250g/10oz shortcrust dough (chilled fresh dough)
flour for the work surface
fat for the oven dish
750g/1lb 10oz oyster mushrooms
salt
freshly ground black pepper
1 tsp herbes de Provence
150g/5¹/₂oz crème fraîche
100g/4oz Appenzeller cheese, freshly grated
handful of French parsley, finely chopped

1. Heat the olive oil in a frying pan. Add the chopped onion and sauté until transparent.
2. Preheat the oven to 220°C/425°F/Gas Mark 7.
3. Roll the dough out on a floured work surface. Grease a springform 26cm/ 10¹/₂ inches in diameter and line it with the dough, making the rim about 4cm/1¹/₂ inches high, and pricking the base with a fork several times. Bake on the centre shelf of the oven for 10 minutes.
4. Meanwhile, wash the oyster mushrooms and cut them into thin strips. Add them to the onions in the pan and sauté until all the liquid has evaporated. Season generously with salt, pepper and herbs, then leave to cool for a short while.
5. Gently fold the crème fraîche and grated cheese into the mushrooms. Spread the mixture evenly over the pastry and bake for a further 15 minutes. Before serving, garnish with the parsley.

Accompaniment: a crispy mixed green salad.

SPINACH QUICHE

SERVES 4 ■

Preparation and cooking time: 35 minutes
Kcal per portion: 545
P = 10g, F = 40g, C = 32g

30g/1oz butter
1 onion, chopped
300g/10oz frozen spinach
salt
freshly ground black pepper
freshly grated nutmeg
250g/8oz short-crust pastry dough (chilled fresh dough)
flour for the work surface
fat for the oven dish
150g/5¹/₂oz crème fraîche with herbs
2 eggs

1. Heat the butter in a pan, add the diced onion and sauté until transparent. Add the spinach and allow it to thaw, stirring occasionally. Season with salt, pepper and nutmeg.
2. Preheat the oven to 200°C/400°F/Gas Mark 6.
3. Roll the dough out on a floured work surface. Grease a springform tin 26cm/ 10¹/₂ inches in diameter and line it with the dough, making the edge about 4cm/1¹/₂ inches high, and pricking the base with a fork several times. Bake on the centre shelf of the oven for 10 minutes.
4. Drain the excess liquid off the spinach, then mix it with the crème fraîche and eggs. Spread the mixture over the pastry base and bake for a further 15 minutes.
Accompaniment: tomato salad with fresh basil.
Recommended drink: beer or dry white wine.

CHEESE AND LEEK QUICHE

SERVES 4 ■

Preparation and cooking time: 45 minutes
Kcal per portion: 720
P = 30g, F = 46g, C = 40g

250g/8oz short-crust pastry dough (chilled fresh dough)
fat for the oven dish
500g/1lb 2oz leeks
salt
2 eggs
200g/7oz Gouda cheese, grated
250g/8oz cream cheese
1 tbsp cornflour
freshly ground black pepper

1. Preheat the oven to 200°C/400°F/Gas Mark 6.
2. Roll the dough out on a floured work surface. Grease a springform 26cm/ 10¹/₂ inches in diameter and line it with the dough, making the edge about 3cm/1¹/₄ inches high, and pricking the base with a fork several times. Bake on the centre shelf of the oven for 10 minutes.
3. Meanwhile, clean and wash the leeks, slice them into rings and blanch in boiling salted water for 5 minutes. Rinse with ice-cold water and drain well.
4. Combine the eggs with the grated cheese, the cream cheese and the cornflour. Then stir in the chopped leek and season with salt and pepper.
5. Place the leek and cheese mixture in the prebaked pastry base and bake on the centre shelf of the oven for about 30 minutes at 200°C/ 400°F/Gas Mark 6.
Recommended drink: a young wine, or beer.

MILLET RISOTTO WITH SALAMI

SERVES 4 ■

Preparation and cooking time: 30 minutes
Kcal per portion: 520
P = 19g, F = 35g, C = 27g

30g/1oz butter
1 onion, chopped
150g/5¹/₂oz millet
500ml/16 fl oz tomato juice
salt
freshly ground black pepper
200g/7oz salami, cut into ¹/₂ cm/¹/₄-inch thick slices
handful of fresh parsley, chopped
80g/3¹/₂oz Emmental, grated

1. Melt the butter in a pan, add the chopped onion and fry until transparent. Then add the millet and stir until all the grains are coated in fat.

> **TIP**
>
> *Millet risotto without meat or fish makes an excellent accompaniment or stuffing for poultry or vegetables.*

2. Pour over the tomato juice and bring the mixture to the boil. Then cover and cook for 20 minutes over a low heat. Season generously with salt and pepper.
3. Skin the salami and dice it finely. Place in a dry, non-stick pan and fry until crispy.
4. Combine the diced salami, parsley, cheese and cooked millet. Season once more to taste.
Accompaniment: chinese cabbage salad with a yoghurt and chive dressing.
Recommended drink: cider.

Microwave Recipes

*A*lthough the ingredients contained in this book will delight wholefood enthusiasts, there is no need to exclude modern conveniences from healthy cooking. Pasta and rice dishes, pizzas and quiches can all be made successfully in the microwave. Of course, you have to know how to use and make the best of your equipment. Lasagne verde and tender seafood, for instance, are an ideal combination for the microwave, as they both reach perfection at exactly the same moment. It is important to be economical with salt, and to stir sauces, vegetables and risottos occasionally while cooking. If you have a combination oven and use it for baking and grilling, ovenproof dishes should be used to avoid any mishaps. Incidentally, it is generally better for containers to be wide and flat rather than narrow and tall.

Pizza with Courgette and Salami Topping (see recipe on page 104)

LASAGNE WITH SPINACH AND CHEESE FILLING

SERVES 4 ■■
Combination microwave oven
Preparation and cooking time: 45 minutes
Kcal per portion: 810
P = 37g, F = 36g, C = 77g

1 onion
100g/4oz uncooked, lean ham
5 tbsps olive oil
300g/10oz frozen, chopped spinach
salt
freshly ground black pepper
freshly grated nutmeg
1 large can tomatoes (800g/1³/4lbs)
1 chopped garlic clove
1 tsp thyme leaves, stems discarded
250g/8oz Ricotta or quark
100g/4oz freshly grated Parmesan
9 uncooked sheets of lasagne

Thaw the frozen spinach in the microwave for 5 minutes at 180 watts.

Arrange the lasagne, ricotta and ham mixture and the spinach in alternate layers in a lasagne dish.

1. Peel the onion and dice both the ham and the onion finely. Place both in a microwave dish with 2 tbsps oil. Fry for 3-4 minutes at 600 watts until transparent.
2. Remove the frozen spinach from the packet, place it on a plate and thaw for 5 minutes at 180 watts. Season with salt, pepper and nutmeg and set aside.
3. Chop the tomatoes and place them with their juice in a microwave dish. Add the garlic and thyme and season with salt and pepper. Cover and cook for 5 minutes at 600 watts.
4. Stir the Ricotta or quark into the onion and ham mixture, add the Parmesan, and season with salt and pepper.
5. Preheat the oven on a conventional setting to 200°C.
6. Grease an ovenproof dish which is also suitable for the microwave with 1 tbsp oil. Lay 3 sheets of lasagne in the base. First cover with half of the Ricotta and ham mixture, then spread over half of the spinach. Add another layer of 3 sheets of lasagne, covering it with another layer of Ricotta and ham, followed by another layer of spinach. Finally top with the remaining lasagne. Pour over the tomato sauce and sprinkle with the remaining Parmesan and oil.
7. Cover and cook for 15-18 minutes at 600 watts and 200°C (180°C in a fan-assisted oven) on the centre shelf of the oven. Five minutes before the end of the cooking time, remove the lid. Allow the lasagne to stand for about 5 minutes before cutting.
Recommended wine:
a light, Italian red wine, such as Lambrusco.

CANNELLONI WITH AUBERGINE FILLING

SERVES 4 ■■
Combination microwave oven
Preparation and cooking time: 1 hour
Kcal per portion: 995
P = 34g, F = 48g, C = 93g

FOR THE FILLING:
1 medium-sized aubergine (500g/1lb 2oz)
2 tbsps chopped onion
1 chopped garlic clove
2 tbsps olive oil
200g/7oz sausage filling (Bratwurst)
1 beefsteak tomato
4 tbsps cream
salt
freshly ground black pepper
1 tsp thyme leaves, plucked from the stem

FOR THE TOMATO SAUCE:
500g/1lb 2oz ripe tomatoes
1 chopped garlic clove
3 tbsps olive oil
125ml/4 fl oz red wine
1 sprig rosemary
salt
freshly ground black pepper

PLUS:
a 150g/5¹/2oz ball of Mozzarella
12 ready-made cannelloni
oil for the oven dish

1. Prick the aubergine in several places with a fork, place it on a plate and cook in the microwave for 8-10 minutes at 600 watts, turning once.
2. Meanwhile, place the diced onion and garlic with the oil in a microwave dish and fry for 2-3 minutes at 600 watts, uncovered, until transparent. Add the sausage and cook for a further 2-3 minutes at 600 watts.
3. Meanwhile, halve the aubergine, scrape out the flesh, and mash it with a fork. Blanch the tomatoes, then peel, seed and dice them. Add the aubergine flesh, the cream and the tomatoes to the fried sausage filling. Season with salt, pepper and thyme, cover and cook for 3-4 minutes at 600 watts.
4. To make the tomato sauce, wash and chop the tomatoes and place them in a microwave dish together with the garlic, oil, red wine and rosemary. Season with salt and pepper, cover and cook for 8 minutes at 600 watts. Then rub the mixture through a sieve.
5. Preheat the oven on a conventional setting to 200°C.
6. Dice the Mozzarella finely and stir half the quantity into the aubergine and meat mixture.
7. Fill the cannelloni with the filling using a teaspoon. Lay them alongside one another in a greased microwave dish and cover evenly with the tomato sauce. Top with the remaining diced Mozzarella, cover and bake on the centre shelf of the oven for 15-18 minutes at 600 watts and 200°C (180°C for fan-assisted ovens). Remove the covering from the dish 5 minutes before the end of the cooking time.
Recommended wine:
an Italian red, such as Montepulciano.

> **TIP**
> *Minced meat may be used instead of sausagemeat. This filling may also be used to make a lasagne.*

PIZZA WITH SPINACH AND GOAT'S CHEESE

SERVES 4 ▪▪
Combination microwave oven
Preparation and cooking time: 30 minutes
Rising time: 45 minutes
Kcal per portion: 595
P = 27g, F = 36g, C = 38g

FOR THE PIZZA DOUGH:
200g/7oz flour
salt
10g/¼oz fresh yeast
125ml/4 fl oz lukewarm water
1 tbsp olive oil

FOR THE TOPPING:
500g/1lb 2oz young spinach leaves
salt
200g/7oz semi-hard goat's cheese
1 ball of Mozzarella (150g/5½oz)
1 chopped shallot
1 chopped garlic clove
3 tbsps chopped walnuts
2 tbsps walnut oil
2 tbsps olive oil

PLUS:
oil for the baking sheet

1. Place the flour and salt in a bowl, make a well in the centre and crumble in the yeast. Combine with a little lukewarm water, cover with a cloth and leave to rise in a warm place for 15 minutes. Then pour in the oil and the rest of the water, kneading the mixture to make a firm dough that no longer sticks to the base of the bowl. Cover and again leave to rise in a warm place for 30 minutes.
2. Meanwhile, sort the spinach and wash it thoroughly. While still wet, place it in a sufficiently large microwave dish, season with salt, cover and cook for 2-3 minutes at 600 watts. Drain in a colander and cool.
3. Crumble the goat's cheese, dice the Mozzarella finely and combine the two.
4. Preheat the oven to a conventional setting of 220°C.

Add 1 tbsp olive oil to the starter.

Spread the cheese mixture evenly over the spinach.

5. Roll the pizza dough out to make a rectangle 35 x 30cm/14 x 12 inches in size, placing it on a greased baking sheet. Cover the base with spinach leaves, then scatter the diced shallot and onion, the cheese and the chopped walnuts on top. Sprinkle over the oil and bake for 13-15 minutes at 180 watts and 220°C (200°C for fan-assisted ovens). Divide into slices and serve immediately.
Recommended wine:
a full-bodied white wine or a dry, full-bodied red wine.

> **TIP**
> *The stronger the flavour of the goat's cheese, the tastier the pizza. If you prefer a milder taste, use cream cheese made from goat's milk, either with or without herbs.*

PIZZA WITH COURGETTE AND SALAMI TOPPING

Photo, page 100/101

SERVES 4 ▪
Combination microwave oven
Preparation and cooking time: 30 minutes
Rising time: 45 minutes
Kcal per portion: 490
P = 22g, F = 25g, C = 45g

FOR THE PIZZA DOUGH:
200g/7oz flour
salt
10g/¼oz fresh yeast
125ml/4 fl oz lukewarm water
1 tbsp olive oil

FOR THE TOPPING:
3 courgettes
2 balls of Mozzarella (150g/5½oz each)
380g/14oz tomato and herb pizza topping (available in a jar)
100g/4oz salami, sliced thinly
1 tsp fresh thyme leaves, plucked from the stem
2 tbsps olive oil

PLUS:
oil for the baking sheet

1. Place the flour and salt in a bowl, make a well in the centre and crumble in the yeast. Combine with a little lukewarm water, cover with a cloth and leave to rise in a warm place for 15 minutes. Then pour in the oil and the rest of the water, kneading the mixture to make a firm dough that no longer sticks to the base of the bowl. Cover and leave to rise in a warm place for a further 30 minutes.
2. Slice the courgettes and the halved Mozzarella balls thinly.
3. Preheat the combination oven to a conventional setting of 220°C.
4. Roll the pizza dough out to make a rectangle 35 x 30cm/14 x 12 inches in size,

Truly Italian: courgettes go well with pizza.

and place it on an oiled baking sheet. Prick the dough in several places with a fork, cover it with the tomato, and top with the courgette, salami and Mozzarella slices, arranged in alternate rows, each slice overlapping the next. Finally sprinkle over the thyme leaves and the oil.
5. Bake for 14-16 minutes at 180 watts and 220°C (200°C for a fan-assisted oven) on the centre shelf.
Recommended wine:
a light Italian red wine.

> **TIP**
> *Only with a combination oven is it possible to prepare a home-made pizza from start to finish so quickly that you can be serving it to your guests or family within half an hour.*

CHINESE VEGETABLE FLAN

SERVES 4 ■

Combination microwave oven
Preparation and cooking time: 30 minutes
Kcal per portion: 515
P = 12g, F = 41g, C = 20g

200g/7oz frozen puff dough

FOR THE FILLING:
300g/10oz frozen mixed Chinese vegetables
3 eggs
200ml/7 fl oz cream
20ml/1½ tbsps rice wine or dry sherry
1 tbsp soy sauce
1 garlic clove, chopped
generous pinch of ground ginger
½ tsp curry powder
salt
freshly ground black pepper

PLUS:
2 tsps sesame seeds for garnishing

Place the sheets of pastry on a baking sheet and thaw in the microwave.

Roll the dough out into a round base.

Finally scatter the sesame seeds over the flan.

1. Place the sheets of puff pastry side by side in the microwave oven and thaw for 2-3 minutes at 180 watts.
2. Then preheat the oven to a conventional setting of 200°C.
3. Brush the sheets of dough with a little water, place them one on top of the other, and roll them out to make a circle

> **TIP**
>
> ***The vegetables will thaw and cook while the pastry is baking. With a glass of sherry, this flan makes an hors d'oeuvre for 6-8 people.***

with a diameter of 24cm/8½ inches. Rinse a shallow microwave dish (20cm/8 inches in diameter) with cold water, then line the inside of the dish with the dough.
4. Spread the frozen vegetables evenly over the dough.
5. Whisk the eggs and combine them with the cream, rice wine or sherry and soy sauce. Season with garlic, ginger, curry powder, salt and pepper and spread the mixture over the vegetables. Garnish with sesame seeds.
6. Bake on the centre shelf of the oven for 18-20 minutes at 360 watts and 200°C (180°C for fan-assisted ovens). Before cutting, leave to stand for 5-10 minutes.
Recommended drink:
dry sherry (fino).

CEP FLAN

SERVES 6-8 ■ ■
Combination microwave oven
Preparation and cooking time: 1 hour
Standing time: 30 minutes
Kcal per portion, serving 6: 515
P = 10g, F = 36g, C = 35g

FOR THE DOUGH:
200g/7oz flour
salt
100g/4oz chilled butter
2-3 tbsps ice-cold water

FOR THE FILLING:
500g/1lb 2oz fresh ceps
80g/3oz butter
2 small shallots, chopped
20g/¾oz flour
125ml/4 fl oz cream
125ml/4 fl oz milk
salt
freshly ground black pepper
2 tbsps chopped fresh herbs (such as parsley, chervil, tarragon and basil)
2 egg yolks
2 egg whites

PLUS:
flour for the work surface
fat for the oven dish
1 egg yolk for glazing

1. Place the flour and salt on a baking sheet, add the butter, in small pieces, and chop into the mixture with a broad-bladed knife. Add as much ice-cold water as necessary, and briskly knead into a smooth dough. Wrap in clingfilm and place in the refrigerator for 30 minutes.
2. Clean the ceps, wash them if necessary, and slice them finely. Place 30g/1oz butter with the diced shallots in a large microwave dish and fry for 2-3 minutes at 600 watts until transparent. Add the mushrooms and cook without a lid for 6-8 minutes at 600 watts, stirring occasionally.
3. Melt the remaining butter for 1 minute at 600 watts, then stir in the flour and cook for a further 1 minute

Scatter the pieces of butter over the flour and chop into the mixture using a broad-bladed knife.

at 600 watts. Pour over the cream and milk, combine the ingredients thoroughly and cook the mixture for 3-4 minutes at 600 watts. Then stir it well with an egg whisk and season generously with salt, pepper and herbs.
4. Preheat the oven to a conventional setting of 200°C.
5. When the mushroom mixture has cooled a little, mix it with the egg yolks and the béchamel sauce. Beat the egg whites until they form stiff peaks, then fold them gently into the mixture.
6. Roll the dough out on a floured baking sheet until it forms a circle with a diameter of 28cm/11¼ inches. Use the dough to line the inside of a greased spring-form suitable for the microwave, 24cm/9½ inches in diameter. Prick the base in several places using a fork. Then fill the pastry case with the mushroom mixture and spread the whisked egg yolk over the top. Bake for 15-18 minutes at 180 watts and 200°C (180°C for a fan-assisted oven). Before cutting, leave to stand for at least 10 minutes.

Recommended wine:
a fruity white wine, such as a Riesling from Alsace.

Slimline Cookery

*N*ot so long ago, people were trying to persuade us that pasta and all good things made from grains made us fat. War was declared on carbohydrates. Yet times have changed, and the influence of international cuisine has made its mark. A balanced low-calorie diet also requires complex carbohydrates, and these are found in pasta, rice, millet, and buckwheat. The recipes contained in this chapter reveal how to prepare such dishes, including low-calorie feasts such as Mixed Sprout Risotto or Wholewheat Pasta with Wild Herbs, Sweet-and-Sour Rice, and Chinese Stir-Fry with Bean Threads. Italy contributes fusilli, penne, spaghetti and farfalle. Wholefood cuisine also includes low-calorie recipes such as Millet Risotto, and Wholewheat Pizza.

Spaghetti with Seafood
(see recipe on page 110)

WHOLEWHEAT PASTA WITH WILD HERBS

SERVES 4 ■
Preparation and cooking time: 20 minutes
Kcal per portion: 225
P = 11g, F = 9g, C = 33g

200g/7oz wholewheat
  spaghetti
salt
100g/4oz mixed wild herbs
  (such as young dandelion,
  sorrel, rocket
  and daisy)
20g/³/₄oz butter
1 shallot, chopped
1 garlic clove, chopped
salt
freshly ground black pepper
2 tbsps grated Parmesan
30g/1oz roasted sunflower
  seeds

1. Cook the wholewheat pasta in 2l/3½ pints boiling salted water, in accordance with the instructions on the packet, until it is al dente.
2. Meanwhile, wash the wild herbs. Sort them, removing any tough stems and leaves, then chop roughly. It is essential to use fresh herbs, since this is what will determine the flavour of the dish.
3. Heat the butter in a large, non-stick pan, add the shallots and diced garlic and fry until transparent. Then add the wild herbs, season with salt and pepper, and ensure the herbs are coated in melted butter.
4. Pour the pasta into a sieve, drain well and then place immediately in the pan with the herbs. Scatter over the Parmesan. Using two wooden spoons, gently combine the whole mixture. Serve on preheated plates and serve garnished with the roasted sunflower seeds.

Roast the sunflower seeds gently in a pan.

Cook the wholewheat spaghetti in 2l/3½ pints boiling water until al dente.

Sauté the diced garlic and shallots in the hot butter until transparent.

Place the cooked spaghetti in the pan and combine gently with the wild herbs.

SPAGHETTI WITH SEAFOOD

Photo, page 108/109

SERVES 4 ■ ■
Preparation and cooking time: 45 minutes
Kcal per portion: 480
P = 45g, F = 16g, C = 34g

1kg/2¼ lbs mixed shellfish
  (clams, mussels)
200g/7oz fresh prawns
few small squid
4 tbsps olive oil
200g/7oz spaghetti
salt
1 garlic clove, chopped
juice of ½ lemon
1-2 tbsps chopped fresh
  parsley
freshly ground black pepper

1. Scrub and wash the shellfish thoroughly; throw away all shells that have already opened. Peel the prawns, clean the squid and chop them into fine rings.
2. Heat 2 tbsps olive oil in a large saucepan. Place the shellfish in the pan while they are still dripping wet. Cover and cook for about 5-8 minutes, shaking the pan frequently; then remove the clams and mussels from their shells.
3. Cook the spaghetti in 2l/3½ pints boiling salted water for about 10 minutes until al dente.
4. Meanwhile, heat the remaining oil in a large saucepan, add the chopped garlic and sauté for a few minutes. Then add the seafood and simmer over a medium heat for 4-5 minutes. Sprinkle with lemon juice and parsley.
5. Drain the spaghetti well in a colander and place it in the pan with the seafood. Mix thoroughly and season with pepper.

SPAGHETTI WITH MUSHROOMS

SERVES 2 ■
Preparation and cooking time: 20 minutes
Kcal per portion: 320
P = 11g, F = 10g, C = 36g

100g/4oz spaghetti
salt
250g/8oz mushrooms
20g/³/₄oz butter or
  margarine
1 large shallot, chopped
125ml/4 fl oz white wine
freshly ground black pepper
small handful of fresh
  parsley
1 tsp grated horseradish

1. Cook the spaghetti in 1l/1¾ pints salted water for about 10 minutes until al dente.
2. Meanwhile, clean the mushrooms, wash them if necessary, and slice them thinly.

> **TIP**
>
> *If the horseradish is from a jar, it should be stirred into the spaghetti along with the parsley.*

3. Heat the fat in a non-stick pan, add the shallots and sauté until transparent. Then add the mushrooms and stir-fry the mixture over a medium heat. Pour over the wine and season with salt and pepper. Cover and simmer for 2-3 minutes, then remove the lid and boil over a high heat to reduce some of the liquid.
4. Drain the spaghetti in a colander before adding them to the mushrooms. Sprinkle over the parsley, finely chopped, and combine the ingredients thoroughly. Place on two heated plates and serve garnished with horseradish.

FUSILLI WITH TUNA AND CAPERS

SERVES 2 ■
Preparation time:
20 minutes
Kcal per portion: 555
P = 27g, F = 17g, C = 67g

200g/7oz fusilli (spirals)
salt
1 tbsp oil
1 shallot, chopped
1 garlic clove, chopped
2 anchovies, rinsed with
*   water*
1 can of tuna in natural
*   juice (180g/6½oz fish*
*   weight)*
50g/2oz capers
freshly ground black pepper
1-2 tbsps pasta cooking water
1 tbsp chopped fresh parsley

1. Cook the fusilli in 2l/3½ pints boiling salted water for about 15 minutes until al dente.
2. Meanwhile, heat the oil in a non-stick saucepan, add the diced shallot and garlic and fry until transparent.
3. Purée the anchovies and two-thirds of the tuna using a mixer. Place the purée in the pan, heat through briefly, then add the capers and the remaining tuna, broken into pieces.
4. Drain the pasta in a sieve, retaining some of the cooking water. Stir the pasta into the tuna sauce, preferably using two wooden forks, adding a little cooking water if necessary. Serve garnished with parsley.

Fry the chopped garlic and shallots in a sauté pan until transparent.

Purée two thirds of the tuna and the anchovies before heating.

Add the capers and the remainder of the tuna to the hot fish purée.

Mix the cooked fusilli with the tuna sauce.

SPAGHETTI WITH COURGETTES AND TOMATOES

SERVES 4 ■
Preparation time:
30 minutes
Kcal per portion: 290
P = 11g, F = 7g, C = 44g

4 small courgettes
4 ripe beefsteak tomatoes
1 chopped garlic clove
1 tbsp chopped onion
piece of dried pepper
2 tbsps olive oil
salt
freshly ground black pepper
200g/7oz spaghetti
6-8 finely chopped basil
*   leaves*

1. Cut the ends off the courgettes and wash them. Slice them first lengthways, then crossways into narrow strips. Blanch and peel the tomatoes, remove the stalk bases and seeds, and chop the flesh.
2. Using a high-sided frying pan, sauté the diced garlic and onion with the crushed pepper in the olive oil over a medium heat until transparent. Then add the courgette strips, season with salt and pepper and stir-fry until they are lightly browned.
3. Meanwhile, bring 2l/3½ pints salted water to the boil in a large saucepan. Add the spaghetti and cook for 8-10 minutes until al dente.
4. Add the diced tomato to the courgettes and sauté the mixture for a few more minutes. Finally add the drained pasta and combine it thoroughly with the vegetables. Season once more with salt and pepper and serve garnished with basil.

WHOLEWHEAT PASTA WITH SPINACH AND SESAME

SERVES 2 ■
Preparation time:
25 minutes
Kcal per portion: 295
P = 13g, F = 12g, C = 34g

300g/10oz fresh, young
*   spinach*
salt
100g/4oz wholewheat
*   tagliatelle*
1 tbsp olive oil
1 garlic clove, chopped
freshly ground black pepper
20g/¾oz sesame seeds

1. Clean and wash the spinach thoroughly, then drain it well in a sieve. Blanch briefly in a little boiling salted water, then drain once more.
2. Bring 1l/1¾ pints salted water to the boil in a saucepan. Add the pasta and cook according to the instructions on the packet until it is al dente. Transfer to a colander and drain well.
3. Meanwhile, heat the olive oil in a non-stick, high-sided frying pan, add the garlic clove and fry until transparent. Then add the spinach, season with pepper and sauté briefly.
4. Roast the sesame seeds in another, dry pan until golden brown.
5. Add the pasta to the spinach and combine the ingredients gently in the pan. Serve on to two plates and garnish with the roasted sesame seeds.

> **TIP**
> *To save time, use half a packet (150g/5½oz) frozen spinach.*

PIZZA WITH SHRIMPS

SERVES 4 ■■
Preparation and cooking time: 30 minutes
Rising time: 45 minutes
Kcal per portion: 290
P = 6g, F = 12g, C = 38g

FOR THE DOUGH:
200g/7oz strong plain flour
*   pinch of salt*
10g/¹⁄₄oz fresh yeast
about 125ml/4 fl oz
*   lukewarm water*
1 tsp olive oil

FOR THE TOPPING:
2 tbsps olive oil
1 tbsp oregano
1 jar of pizza topping with
*   tomatoes and herbs*
300g/10oz shrimps, freshly
*   shelled*
1 garlic clove, chopped
1 tbsp finely chopped fresh
*   basil*
salt
freshly ground black pepper
fat for the baking sheet

1. Place the flour and salt in a bowl, make a well in the centre and crumble in the yeast. Mix with a little water, cover with a cloth and leave to rise in a warm place for 15 minutes. Then pour in the oil and the remaining water, and knead the mixture to make a smooth dough that no longer sticks to the base of the bowl. Cover and leave to rise in a warm place for a further 30 minutes.
2. Preheat the oven to 250°C/475°F/Gas Mark 9.
3. Divide the pizza dough into 4 small balls and roll each out into a circle of about 15cm/6 inches in diameter. Raise the edges of the dough slightly using the fingers. Place the circles on a greased baking sheet; sprinkle with olive oil and some of the oregano. Prebake on the centre shelf of the oven for 12-15 minutes.
4. Combine the tomato with the shrimps, seasoning with

Knead the dough until it no longer sticks to the base of the bowl.

Raise the edges of the dough slightly using the fingers.

After 15 minutes in the oven, spread the shrimp topping over the pizzas.

the remaining oregano, garlic and basil. Add salt and pepper to taste. Spread the mixture evenly over the pizzas and bake on the top shelf of the oven for a further 4-5 minutes. Serve immediately.

PEPPER PIZZA

SERVES 4 ■■
Preparation and cooking time: 1 hour
Rising time: 45 minutes
Kcal per portion: 380
P = 14g, F = 17g, C = 41g

FOR THE DOUGH:
200g/7oz strong plain flour
pinch of salt
10g/¹⁄₄oz fresh yeast
about 125ml/4 fl oz
*   lukewarm water*

FOR THE TOPPING:
3 red peppers
1 large onion
1 garlic clove
2 tbsps olive oil
a sprig of thyme
salt
freshly ground black pepper
1 tsp balsamic vinegar
1 ball of Mozzarella
*   (150g/5¹⁄₂oz)*
fat for the baking sheet

1. Place the flour and salt in a bowl, make a well in the centre and crumble in the yeast. Mix with a little water, cover with a cloth and leave to rise in a warm place for 15 minutes. Then pour in the oil and the remaining water and knead the mixture to make a smooth dough that no longer sticks to the base of the bowl. Cover and leave to rise in a warm place for a further 30 minutes.
2. Meanwhile, to make the topping, wash the peppers, cut them in half, remove the stalks and seeds, and slice them into fine strips. Peel the onion and slice it finely using a cucumber slicer. Peel the garlic clove and chop finely.
3. Heat the oil in a non-stick pan, add the onion and garlic and fry until transparent. Then add the pepper strips and the thyme and stir-fry for a few minutes. Season with salt and pepper, cover, and simmer over a low heat for about 25-30 minutes. Remove the pan from the heat, remove the sprig of

Peppers are good summer vegetables.

thyme, season with vinegar and add more salt and pepper to taste.
4. Preheat the oven to 220°C/425°F/Gas Mark 7.
5. Roll out the pizza dough to make a circle 26cm/10¹⁄₂ inches in diameter, raising the rim slightly using the fingers. Place on a greased baking sheet and cover with the pepper mixture. Dice the Mozzarella finely and scatter it over the top.
6. Bake on the centre shelf of the oven for about 20 minutes. If desired, serve garnished with chopped herbs.

> **TIP**
>
> *Pepper Pizza may be served as a meal for 4 with a salad, but it can also be divided into small portions as an hors d'oeuvre or appetizer for 8-10 people. Unlike many other pizzas, this pizza is also delicious eaten cold.*

TOMATO RISOTTO WITH BLACK OLIVES

SERVES 2   ■
Preparation and cooking time: 35 minutes
Kcal per portion: 320
P = 6g, F = 11g, C = 48g

2 beefsteak tomatoes
1 tbsp olive oil
1 small onion, chopped
1 garlic clove, chopped
100g/4oz Italian risotto rice
salt
1 tsp tomato purée
250ml/8 fl oz water
1 sprig of basil
10 black olives

After blanching the tomatoes, peel them using a sharp knife.

1. Blanch and peel the tomatoes, remove the stalk bases and the seeds and dice the flesh.
2. Heat the oil in a sauté pan, add the diced onion and garlic and fry until transparent.

Add the diced tomato to the fried rice.

TIP

Risotto should be eaten as soon as it is cooked. It should on no account stand for too long, as it will become too solid and also lose its flavour.
If desired, freshly grated Parmesan may be stirred into the mixture before serving.
A true risotto is made with short-grain rice.
If you prefer your risotto al dente, use long-grain rice.

Slowly pour the water over the tomato and rice mixture.

Stir in first the rice, followed by the chopped tomato. Season with salt. Stir in the tomato purée and gradually pour in the water, stirring constantly. Cook for about 20 minutes, ensuring that the rice is kept boiling vigorously.
3. Pluck the basil leaves from their stem, wash and dry them, then cut them into thin strips. Stone the black olives, cut them into small pieces and stir them into the risotto. Serve immediately.

WHOLEWHEAT PIZZA WITH TUNA, ONIONS AND CAPERS

SERVES 4   ■ ■
Preparation and cooking time: 30 minutes
Rising time: 1 hour
Kcal per portion: 400
P = 17g, F = 19g, C = 37g

FOR THE DOUGH:
150g/5½oz strong
    wholewheat flour
50g/2oz wheatmeal
pinch of salt
10g/¼oz fresh yeast
about 200ml/6 fl oz
    lukewarm water
1 tsp oil

FOR THE TOPPING:
1 large onion
200g/7oz ready-made
    tomato and herb pizza
    topping
1 garlic clove, chopped
salt
freshly ground black pepper
1 x 200g/7oz can of tuna in
    brine
30g/1oz capers

PLUS:
2 tbsps olive oil
oil for the baking sheet

1. Mix the wheat flour, wheatmeal and salt in a bowl, make a well in the centre and crumble in the yeast. Stir in a little water, cover

TIP

Of course this wholewheat pizza dough tastes good with any topping.

with a cloth and leave to rise in a warm place for 15 minutes. Then pour in the oil and the remaining water. Knead the mixture to make a smooth dough that no longer sticks to the base of the bowl. Cover and again leave to rise in a warm place for a further 45 minutes.

Slice the onions into wafer-thin rings using a cucumber slicer.

First coat the pizza bases with the tomato sauce, then arrange the onion rings, the capers and the tuna fish on top.

2. Preheat the oven to 220°C/425°F/Gas Mark 7.
3. Peel the onions and slice them very finely using a cucumber slicer. Season the tomato generously with garlic, salt and pepper.
4. Once the dough has risen, shape it into four small balls and roll each out into a circle 15cm/6 inches in diameter. Make the edges slightly thicker using the fingers. Place the circles on a greased baking sheet and cover them with the tomatoes. Spread the finely sliced onion rings over the top. Break the tuna into pieces and arrange both the tuna and the capers on top of the onion. Finally sprinkle with oil. Bake for about 20 minutes on the centre shelf of the oven. Serve immediately.

MILLET RISOTTO WITH WILD MUSHROOMS

SERVES 2 ■
Preparation and cooking time: 40 minutes
Kcal per portion: 280
P = 9g, F = 11g, C = 36g

250g/8oz mixed wild
   mushrooms
1 onion
1 carrot
1 small parsnip
20g/³/₄oz butter or
   margarine
100g/4oz millet
salt
freshly ground black pepper
grated, untreated orange
   rind
250ml/8 fl oz chicken stock
1 tbsp chopped fresh parsley

1. Clean the mushrooms, wash them if they are dirty, and cut them into strips, not

> ### TIP
> *If calories are not too much of a concern, stir a little butter or crème fraîche into the risotto.*

too finely. Peel the onion, scrape and wash the carrot and parsley root, then dice all three vegetables extremely finely.
2. Heat the fat in a saucepan, add the onion, carrot and parsley root or parsnip and sauté them for a few minutes. Then add the mushrooms and stir-fry over a high heat for a further few minutes. Scatter the millet into the pan, seasoning with salt, pepper and orange peel. Pour over the bouillon. Bring the mixture to the boil, then cover and simmer over a low heat for about 25 minutes, stirring occasionally. Finally stir in the chopped parsley.

MIXED SPROUT RISOTTO

SERVES 2 ■
Preparation and cooking time: 35 minutes
Kcal per portion: 275
P = 11g, F = 6g, C = 42g

2 spring onions
100g/4oz mushrooms
1 tbsp oil
100g/4oz short-grain brown
   rice
1 tsp mild curry powder
salt
1 tbsp soy sauce
250ml/8 fl oz vegetable stock
200g/7oz bamboo shoots
handful of soya bean
   sprouts
few sprigs of coriander or
   parsley

1. Clean and wash the spring onions, then slice them finely, including part of the green tops. Clean the mushrooms, wash them if necessary, and slice them finely. Normally it is sufficient to wipe the mushrooms with a piece of absorbent paper.
2. Heat the oil in a pan, add the onions and fry until transparent. Then add the mushrooms, continuing to fry, followed by the rice. Sprinkle over the curry powder, season with salt, and stir in the soy sauce. Slowly pour over the vegetable stock, stirring constantly. Cover and cook.

> ### TIP
> *If you are not counting the calories, stir a little crème fraîche into this nutritious risotto just before serving.*

3. Chop the bamboo shoots finely. After the vegetables have boiled for about 15 minutes, add the bamboo shoots and soya bean

Add the uncooked rice to the mushrooms.

Pour over the soy sauce before adding the vegetable stock.

Boil the risotto for 15 minutes before adding the bamboo shoots and soya bean sprouts.

sprouts. Cook for a further 5 minutes. Serve the risotto on two deep plates and garnish with coriander leaves.

BUCKWHEAT RISOTTO

SERVES 2 ■
Preparation and cooking time: 40 minutes
Kcal per portion: 330
P = 15g, F = 12g, C = 39g

1 small leek
100g/4oz chanterelle
   mushrooms
200g/7oz cauliflower
20g/³/₄oz butter or
   margarine
1 small onion, chopped
1 garlic clove, chopped
80g/3oz buckwheat
100g/4oz frozen peas
piece of dried pepper
generous pinch of ground
   saffron
salt
freshly ground black pepper
250ml/8 fl oz vegetable stock
   (instant)
1 tbsp freshly chopped herbs
   (parsley, chives, chervil,
   basil)
2 tbsps freshly grated
   Parmesan

1. Chop the top off the leek, retaining some of the green leaves. Then cut it in half, wash it thoroughly and slice it finely. Clean the chanterelles, wash them if necessary, then cut them in half. Wash the cauliflower and divide it into tiny florets.
2. Heat the fat, add the diced onion and garlic and fry until transparent. Then add the leek, mushrooms and cauliflower and stir-fry.
3. Scatter the buckwheat and peas into the pan. Season with the crushed pepper, saffron, salt and pepper. Pour over the vegetable stock. Bring once to the boil, then cover and cook over a low heat for about 15 minutes. Finally stir in the herbs and cheese.

PENNE WITH SPRING ONIONS AND SOY SAUCE

SERVES 2 ■
Preparation and cooking time: 30 minutes
Kcal per portion: 520
P = 18g, F = 14g, C = 73g

200g/7oz penne
salt
bunch of spring onions
2 tbsps oil
1 garlic clove, chopped
2 tbsps soy sauce
2 tbsps rice wine or dry
   sherry (fino)
generous pinch of Chinese
   five-spice
generous pinch of lemon
   grass or grated lemon peel
generous pinch of ground
   ginger
2 tbsps yoghurt (3.5% fat)
1 tbsp finely chopped chives

1. Cook the penne in 2l/3½ pints boiling salted water for just under 15 minutes until al dente.
2. Meanwhile, clean and wash the spring onions, then chop them obliquely into thin slices, including some of the green tops.
3. Heat the oil in a wok or sauté pan, add the onions and garlic and stir-fry until the onions are cooked, but

Slice the spring onions at an angle.

Fry the chopped garlic and onion together in a wok until cooked but still crispy.

Stir the penne into the vegetables with 2 tbsps yoghurt.

TIP

Penne are short, narrow, tubular pasta shapes cut obliquely at the ends like quills. Not only do they go well with a whole variety of vegetable, meat and cheese sauces, but they are also suitable for oriental dishes, as this recipe proves.

still crispy. Pour over the soy sauce and rice wine or sherry and season with the Chinese five-spice, the lemon grass or lemon peel, and the ground ginger.
4. Drain the penne well in a colander. Combine the yoghurt and the penne with the vegetables. Heat through once more, stirring frequently. Serve garnished with chives.

PENNE WITH FINE GREEN BEANS AND CHANTERELLES

SERVES 2 ■
Preparation and cooking time: 40 minutes
Kcal per portion: 785
P = 36g, F = 14g, C = 118g

200g/7oz fine green beans
salt
200g/7oz penne
150g/5½oz fresh chanterelles
1 tbsp oil
10g/¼oz butter
1 shallot, chopped
1 garlic clove, chopped
4 tbsps dry white wine
1 tbsp chopped fresh parsley
1 tbsp chopped fresh chervil
freshly ground black pepper

1. Wash the beans and cut off the ends. Bring a generous quantity of salted water to the boil in a large saucepan, add the beans and boil them for a few minutes until they are cooked but still crisp. Remove them with a slotted spoon and dip them straight into ice-cold water so that they retain their attractive green colour.
2. Boil the penne in the water used for cooking the beans for just under 15 minutes until al dente.
3. Meanwhile, clean the mushrooms, wash them if necessary, and chop them in half.
4. Heat the oil and butter in a non-stick, sauté pan, add the chopped onion and garlic and sauté until transparent. Then add the mushrooms and stir-fry for about 5 minutes.
5. Add the beans and pour over the white wine. Boil the mixture briefly, then stir in the herbs and the well-drained penne. Grind black pepper on top.

SEMOLINA RISSOLES

SERVES 4 ■■
Preparation and cooking time: 40 minutes
Kcal per portion: 270
P = 9g, F = 14g, C = 26g

20g/¾oz butter or
   margarine
1 onion, chopped
150g/5½oz wholewheat
   semolina
200ml/6 fl oz vegetable stock
   (instant)
1 egg
1 tsp herb mustard
2 tbsps grated hard cheese,
   such as fairly mature Gouda
1 tbsp chopped fresh herbs
   (parsley, basil, chervil,
   tarragon)
salt
freshly ground black pepper
1 tbsp wholemeal
   breadcrumbs (if required)
2 tbsps oil for frying

1. Heat the fat in a saucepan, add the chopped onion and fry until transparent. Then stir in the semolina and pour over the vegetable stock. Cover and cook over a low heat for about 15-20 minutes, stirring occasionally. Then leave the mixture to cool a little.
2. Add the egg, mustard, cheese and herbs. Season generously with salt and pepper. If the mixture is still too soft, stir in the breadcrumbs.
3. Shape the semolina dough into 8 rissoles. Heat the oil in a non-stick pan and fry the rissoles on both sides over a medium heat for about 4 minutes. Serve with yoghurt and garlic or a tomato sauce and green salad.

CHINESE STIR-FRY WITH BEAN THREADS

SERVES 4 ■■

Preparation and cooking time: 40 minutes
Kcal per portion: 280
P = 20g, F = 7g, C = 30g

150g/5¹/₂oz bean threads
10g/¹/₄oz Chinese cloud ear
  mushrooms
1 leek
2 carrots
1 garlic clove
200g/7oz turkey breast
  fillet
1 tsp cornflour
2 tbsps sesame oil
1 tsp freshly chopped ginger
  root
piece of dried pepper
3 tbsps soy sauce
2 tbsps dry sherry (fino)
125ml/4 fl oz chicken
  bouillon (canned)
salt
freshly ground black pepper
1 tbsp chopped fresh parsley

1. Place the bean threads and the mushrooms in separate bowls and blanch them with boiling water. Leave to soak for 30 minutes.
2. Clean and wash the leek and carrots and slice them thinly. Peel the garlic cloves and chop them finely. Slice the meat into narrow strips and coat in the cornflour.
3. Heat the oil in a wok or a high-sided frying pan. First stir-fry the vegetables on their own, then add the meat and continue frying. Next, stir in the well-drained bean threads and mushrooms, as well as the ginger and crushed pepper. Combine the mixture thoroughly and pour over the soy sauce, sherry and chicken bouillon. Boil vigorously over a high heat until the sauce is creamy. Season with salt and pepper and garnish with parsley.

SWEET-AND-SOUR RICE

SERVES 4 ■■

Preparation and cooking time: 35 minutes
Kcal per portion: 300
P = 5g, F = 10g, C = 44g

200g/7oz parboiled rice
salt
¹/₂ a small pineapple
8 very small shallots
2 tbsps peanut oil
2 tbsps mild curry powder
20ml/1¹/₂ tbsps dry sherry
  (fino)
2 tbsps desiccated coconut
4 finely chopped mint leaves

1. Cook the parboiled rice in a covered pan filled with 500ml/16 fl oz boiling salted water for about 30 minutes over a low heat.
2. While the rice is cooking, peel the pineapple thoroughly, cut out the hard centre and dice the flesh finely. Peel the shallots, cutting any large ones in half.

> **TIP**
>
> *Parboiled rice is a yellowish colour and is husked in such a way that it retains more B vitamins and minerals than white rice. It represents a good alternative to whole-grain rice, although it does contain considerably less fibre.*

3. Heat the peanut oil in a non-stick pan, add the shallots and sauté them for a few minutes. Sprinkle over the curry powder and pour on the sherry.
4. Cover the pan and braise over a low heat for about 10 minutes, shaking the pan occasionally. Then add the

Sprinkle curry powder over the fried shallots and then pour in the sherry.

After 10 minutes, add the pieces of pineapple and continue frying for a short while.

Roast the desiccated coconut in a dry frying pan, stirring constantly.

chopped pineapple and continue cooking for a few more minutes.
5. Stir-fry the desiccated coconut in a dry pan.
6. Place the cooked rice in the pan with the shallots and pineapple, combine thoroughly and add more seasoning if required.
Serve garnished with mint leaves and desiccated coconut.

ORIENTAL NOODLES

SERVES 4 ■■

Preparation and cooking time: 40 minutes
Kcal per portion: 375
P = 22g, F = 17g, C = 29g

500g/1lb 2oz white cabbage
3 tbsps oil
150g/5¹/₂oz tagliatelle
salt
250g/8oz minced beef
2-3 tbsps soy sauce
1 tsp Chinese five-spice
  powder
freshly ground black pepper
few sprigs of coriander or
  parsley

1. Cut out the cabbage heart and shred the cabbage finely using a cucumber slicer or shredder.
2. Heat 2 tbsps oil in a wok or sauté pan, add a handful of cabbage and stir-fry over a medium heat until transparent, ensuring that it does not start to turn brown. Keep adding more cabbage until it has all been used.
3. Bring 1¹/₂ l/2¹/₂ pints salted water to the boil, add the tagliatelle and cook for 5-8 minutes until al dente.
4. When the vegetables are cooked but still crispy, heat the remaining oil in a non-stick pan, add the minced beef and stir-fry.
5. Drain the pasta well in a colander, then stir it into the cabbage, along with the fried beef. Season generously with soy sauce, five-spice powder, salt and pepper. Garnish with coriander or parsley and serve immediately.

Index